STORIES THAT MUST BE TOLD

THE VETERANS' WRITING GROUP
GROUP
SAN DIEGO COUNTY

Book design by Ron Pickett, Vernita Black, and Shara French

ISBN-13: 9781707181254
ISBN-10: 170718125X
BISAC: History / Essays

Veterans' Writing Group San Diego County offers mentorship,
support, and publishing opportunities for veteran writers of
all skill levels.

www.veteranswritinggroup.org

DEDICATION

STORIES THAT MUST BE TOLD, the third book published by the Veterans' Writing Group, is humbly dedicated to two of our writers whom we have lost since the publication of *LISTEN UP! Things I Learned From the Military*: Lawrence Klumas and Frank Sutton,

- Lawrence was an inspiration up until his death and beyond. He gave us the title and the ideas behind this volume.
- Frank was a consistent and strong positive motivation for us. His excitement, his stories, and enthusiasm, and especially his alliterations were highly influential and entertaining for all of our writers. Frank was our last surviving World War II veteran.

Both of these great men made significant contributions to our group and our members.

Fair winds and following seas.

TABLE OF CONTENTS

VIETNAM STORIES

INSPIRATIONAL STORIES

AUTHORS' BIOGRAPHIES

INTRODUCTION

Stories – They are how we save our heritage and maintain our civilization.

"[N]arrative is the oldest and most compelling method of holding someone's attention; everybody wants to be told a story. Always look for ways to convey your information in narrative form." - William Zinsser

Yes, stories are entertainment. Sitting around a fire telling tales is one of the things that distinguished humans from other animals. But there is a far bigger role that they play in our society.

The stories in this book, the third that the Veterans' Writing Group has published, are primarily meant to entertain, but we hope they do much more. The advent of the all-volunteer force in 1973 has led to a separation of the majority of the American public from those who choose to serve in the military. We believe that we have captured a couple dozen slices of military life; stories that describe terror and boredom, friendship and conflict, sacrifice and selfishness.

These are the stories of individuals embedded in large systems. See how they have behaved, what they thought, to stand out from the crowd and to bring about change. Find out how they have "bucked the system" when they felt that they were right.

But mostly, we hope you will enjoy the stories, stories that must be told – before they are lost forever, stories that will entertain and educate.

Several times in the past year I have had someone tell me about an event that happened while they were visiting a friend or relative at one of the local naval hospitals. They found a copy of one of our earlier books and read selections to the hospitalized person. They went on to tell me how meaningful and helpful those stories were to their loved one. Generous donations from San Diego County and a variety of individuals and foundations have helped us donate over 2500 copies of *Away For the Holidays* and *Listen Up! Things I Learned From the Military* to local military hospitals, VA hospitals, the USO, and a variety of veterans' homes. This year we received a sizable donation from Ray and Tamra Brown. This will permit us to expand our outreach and donation programs. Their generosity together with book sales have encouraged us to expand our reach through additional donations of books, adding an oral history project, providing information and coaching to other agencies interested in starting writing groups, and other initiatives that are currently being developed.

We have been greatly assisted in this project by our three editors: J. Randy Davis, Glen Foss, and R. Bruce Rowe. Without their dedication and hard work this project could not have been accomplished.

We invite veterans and others interested in writing to join us for our monthly meeting. Currently, we meet at Veterans' Association of North County (VANC) 1617 Mission Avenue, Oceanside CA on the third Saturday of every month. (Check our web site for updated information.)

If you are interested in learning more about our group and our work or in starting a Veterans' Writing Group, please contact us at: http://www.veteranswritinggroup.org/

Ron Pickett

WHY WE SERVE . . . WHY WE FIGHT

A NEW LIFE
Anissia Asencio

"Do you want to try?" Eduardo mumbled softly over the phone, as if he was scared.
"Do you?" I replied. I needed his assurance before I answered.
"I do babe! I want to have a baby with you!"
"Then yes, I would love to!"

My husband and I had been talking about trying to conceive for months. Living on opposite ends of the coast had only delayed our process; he lived in California while I resided in North Carolina. We had never pictured ourselves in a long-distance relationship before we met. However, we had been married for over a year and together for more, and yet had never lived together. A part of me was glad for this separation, though, because it allotted us time to think to ourselves if having a baby is what we truly wanted.

***

Months passed, and there I was, sitting on our mattress that was on the floor, waiting to hear if Eduardo had gotten good news. We had finally moved in together. After telling the Marine Corps that I was pregnant, it had taken months for me to be stationed in California with my husband. We had only been living together for a week, and now the Corps wanted to deploy him. We were finally in the same state and under the same roof; we could finally experience this pregnancy together; I didn't have to go through it by myself anymore. Or so we thought, and now this. I couldn't cry, even though I wanted to.

I heard Eduardo drive up the driveway, and I rushed to open the door. He looked sad. He walked in our house and went to the kitchen.

"What did they say?" I asked.
"Sorry, babe, I have to go."

The next month, May of 2017, Eduardo left for deployment. We tried to talk everyday but with him in Japan, the huge time difference made it difficult to communicate. When he did call and we talked, it was always short. I was either asleep when he phoned or when I called him, he was getting ready to go to work. And it was unlike when we were long distance before in other ways, too. I was expecting. I was in a new state with a new chain of command, and I had no friends. I hated him for leaving me like this. I didn't understand why he couldn't have just told them no. I mean, I knew it was impossible; we signed a contract and where the Marine Corps needs you, it will send you. All the same, I despised him for going. How could we ever be a family if we were forever living in different places?

One night, I called my mother and asked if she could stay with me because I didn't want to go through this pregnancy alone. She said she wouldn't miss the birth, and that I would never be alone. I cried when she said that. It was soothing to know that my mother would be with me.

***

On July 28th, 2018, my mother drove us to the Camp Pendleton Naval Hospital. I lived ten minutes away from the hospital. I was crying and begging my mom to speed. She insisted she was doing her best. I couldn't stay still in my seat. I needed to get there now! I gripped the seat belt with all my strength. I was cramping, and I was annoyed. My mom was patient and told me to breathe and that everything was going to be okay. I tried looking at my mother to respond, but my vision was no longer useful. My body had gone completely cold, yet I was sweating. How could that be? I hinted to my mother with words that I didn't think I could make it. I had to close my eyes, no matter how much I didn't want to. My eyelids were heavy. My sense of awareness was draining. I closed my eyes and drifted.

"My daughter needs to be seen. She just passed out." That was all I heard my mother say. Honestly, it was all I even cared to hear. The stabbing pains coming from my stomach prevented my paying attention to my mother. I just wanted help. I needed help. I couldn't breathe; I was sweating. I had no energy to take even a step anymore, and my vision was a blur. A male nurse came behind me with a wheelchair, and my mother and he eased me into it. Having someone push me around felt awkward, but because I was enduring pain like no other, I felt grateful for the male nurse. My mother did the talking to the nurses. I couldn't talk, let alone stand. I did, however, manage to retrieve my ID from the bag I had packed months in advance and gave it to the nurse.

They pushed me into a dim room. Like a lost puppy, I looked for my mother. I scanned the room for her, anxiety rising. I didn't want to do this alone. I was scared. All my fears of being alone came rushing fast but then I saw her, and my body loosened up. My mother rubbed my hand while I was being placed on the bed.

One nurse said, "Honey, I need to check you now."

I forced my body to do what she said. "Please let me be fully dilated," I said to myself. Unfortunately, the nurse said I was only four centimeters open, nowhere near the ten centimeters you need to be to begin pushing. However, the contractions were coming fast and hard. It was as if my insides were rearranging themselves, ripping each other apart. I could feel my baby's head. My body was ready. I couldn't wait. My body wasn't letting me. The pain was unbearable. I vomited in the blue bag the nurse handed me when I told her, "I don't think I can do this." I don't know what I was thinking; it was a little late to back out now.

My mother kept repeating that I was doing well while rubbing my back. I thank God for that woman every day now. I started screaming from my body naturally pushing. I tried to calm myself. I couldn't. My baby was coming, whether I was ready or not. The nurses kept telling me to not push and breathe in intervals. I had to push. It was as if all the weight came rushing down. I could no longer feel my body. I was ripping with every push. There was a tear. The doctor and nurses got ready because I could not wait to hit ten centimeters to begin giving birth. I was ready now.

My mother on the sidelines had somehow facetimed my husband. I didn't even notice she had her phone and of all places she could have had her phone facing, she faced it to where the baby would come out. I remember thinking that my husband will be scarred forever watching me give birth from that angle. My mother obviously thought otherwise, because she was holding her phone with one hand in front of the area like her life depended on it. I started pushing. I was sweating. That little bit of makeup I had asked my mother to put on me before heading to the hospital was now a child's painting on my face. I could feel the mascara running down.

I screamed, thinking it would distract me from the pain. People were encouraging me to keep going. "Don't worry, dear, the pain will be over soon," the midwife told me, but I didn't acknowledge anything she was saying.

"I don't care if it will be over soon. I want to not feel it at all." Every push had a new level of pain as the weight was leaning closer and closer. Suddenly the ring of fire came. It was intense, as if I was walking into a burning room. With every step the heat was intensifying, burning the hairs off my body and progressively burning the skin.

My baby's head was most definitely almost out. With each tear came an upgraded version of this burning sensation. It was as if the nurse at the end of the bed had a lighter and was waving it around my body. I was on fire. "One, two, and three, push!" I gripped the bed and pushed. I almost passed out doing it, but I felt this sudden relief and with that came a cry, a little baby's cry.

I had carried this human being for nine months and never heard it make a sound until that very moment. The nurse immediately handed me my baby, all covered in blood, but I didn't care. She was beautiful. To my surprise, her eyes were open. Her eyes looked around the room, gazing and gazing, until they met mine, and I cried. She was in a whole new world she knew nothing about. She was in my arms and she knew me. I thought we were going to be strangers, but we weren't. Her first look in my eyes melted my soul. It was as if she knew I was, and would always be, her protector. I was in love. She was weightless, so small and fragile. *She is my little person; I am now a mother. It's no longer about me anymore. There's nothing I won't do for you, my baby.* I had my mother cut the umbilical cord. After handing my daughter to the nurse to be cleaned, I noticed my mother was still on facetime with my husband. I had completely forgotten that she had even called him. We talked for a few seconds, and I promised him I would call back later.

"Your beautiful baby girl is all cleaned, my dear." The nurse handed me my daughter. While looking at her I kept thinking, I have no idea how to be a mother, but I promised her I would be the best I could. I saw through her eyes that she was going to be a sweetheart. They were small and reminded me of the galaxy, dark and bounded by stars. Her hair was full and as black as tar. Her lips were shaped as the most perfect heart anyone has ever seen. This small person needed me, but not as much as I needed her.

Holding her was priceless. Looking into her eyes gave me clarity. Her cry snapped me into motherhood. The nurses were slowly leaving us alone with my daughter. One started writing on the room's whiteboard. She asked me for my daughter's name, and I smiled. "Her name is Alaina Ava." I looked at my little one in my arms and repeated it. "Alaina Ava," I said, smiling at her. I knew we picked the perfect name for the perfect baby. While I looked at my daughter, the nurse continued writing on the whiteboard.

I handed my daughter to my mother and watched the smile form on my mother's face; her eyes brightened with love as she held her. Seeing my mother in awe of my daughter generated a new grown love for my mother in me. She was my caretaker growing up, and we had been through rough times together. Yet here we were. I was no longer her baby or living under her roof, but I understood her love for me now more than ever before. She took good care of me and gave me the principles to be a parent. Through this woman's mistakes and achievements, I learned valuable lessons. While she held my daughter, I couldn't help but smile and cry. My daughter was to know the greatest woman I know to walk earth.

The nurse had left. I looked up at the whiteboard: "Alaina Ava born at 9:21 p.m. weighing 7 pounds and 19 inches long." Then I heard my daughter's cry, a sharp pain to my heart. I didn't want her to cry. I wanted nothing but happiness for her. "Please don't cry, my dear." My mother gently returned my daughter to me. For the first time, I was going to breastfeed. I was scared. *What do I do? Did my body even produce anything for my love? Will she accept it?* My daughter yearned for help, and I was desperate to give it. She latched fast. I thought giving birth was painful, but breastfeeding is right up there. My mother tried giving me advice. She told me to hold my daughter's head and bring her closer. A part of me didn't want to; this felt taboo. I was against it, until my daughter started feeding. It was as if I could feel the spiritual vines run through me into my daughter. I could see the energy rubbing off and clinging in the air. Breastfeeding was a meditation session that cleansed my mind, body, and soul. My heart grew fonder for my baby. She was grateful. She relaxed. She closed her eyes and focused. She was at peace, so I was at peace, too.

This was the day I gave birth to a life, but it was the day my daughter gave me life, as well.

WORLD WAR II STORIES

A FORCED LANDING IN ITALY
Mark Steinberg

It looked like the entire United States Navy was in Salerno Bay where their guns were lobbing shells to support the Allied troops as they fought their way up the boot of Italy. Our assignment was the Salerno Marshalling Yards.

Puffs of black smoke (flak) appeared as we approached the target. What didn't show were the razor-sharp bits of metal shrapnel that flew off in all directions. The flak became more intense as our flight of six Martin B-26 Marauders crossed the target, and then all hell broke loose. There was an explosion to the rear of our airplane. Staff/Sgt. Sgt. (SSG) Frank Dickenson, the tail gunner, reported on the intercom that it was close because he could smell the smoke.

Immediately, the plane began to shake like a dog shaking a rat. While I assessed the damage, the co-pilot Lt. Eldon Hunsberger hugged his control column, fearful it would break loose. Our bombardier SSG Carl Tackman crawled out of the nose to assist. At 180 miles per hour, the plane was at risk of falling apart, but as the speed decreased, the shaking subsided until we were semi-confident that the airplane was controllable.

Our problem had not gone unnoticed. Two bombers from the same formation positioned themselves on each wing to give added protection against enemy fighters if needed.

With the ship under control, the choices were to either attempt the one-hour flight to our base in north Africa or land on the Italian mainland nearby. Not knowing the condition of the airplane and not being willing to risk the lives of the six crew members, we, the copilot, navigator and I, chose Italy.

At an altitude of 2,000 feet above our Navy, we watched their guns rotate in our direction, close enough that they could have shot us out of the sky. However, they withheld their fire, and we continued descending toward the unknown.

We crossed the beach at an altitude of 500 feet, and luck was with us, for directly ahead was a short fighter strip used by the

Germans only days before. It meant we could land "wheels down" rather than tear up the countryside, not to mention causing damage to the Marauder and possible crew injuries. With full flaps, the approach was just above a stall speed; we touched "terra firma" a few feet beyond a ditch.

With the control column against my chest to keep the nose wheel up, and with three wheels rolling and brakes smoking, we came to rest at the end of the runway. The escort planes made similar landings. After examination, we determined that the explosion had knocked the trim-tab on the vertical stabilizer out of alignment. o fly again, the bird would need a new tail.

With the crew divided between the two escort planes, we raced down the runway, given only a few seconds to salute "Sherry," the plane now deserted, that had brought us safely through a harrowing experience. Returning to Africa, all crew members were no worse for the wear.

A few days later, "Sherry" was again part of our inventory and scheduled for more missions. Command directed me to fly the airplane for a short time after, a procedure intended to prevent future psychological problems. Seeing her back in service was good news and reinforced my belief that the Marauder was indeed an excellent airplane.

USS CUSHING (DD-376) AT THE BATTLE OF GUADALCANAL
November 13–15, 1942
Tom J. Foreman

USS *Cushing* departed Pearl Harbor, headed for the South Pacific area in early October of 1942.

The ship joined a task force and was assigned to act as a screen and plane guard for USS *Enterprise* (CV-6). None of our crew had seen any action, and there were many discussions about what we thought it would be like and when it would happen.

On October 26, 1942, we were involved in the Battle of Santa Cruz. That was very exciting, to say the least; we were able to shoot at many Japanese planes. They were only interested in the carriers—not us. We only had one minor casualty and were very satisfied with the results of our part in the engagement. Since the USS *Hornet* (CV-8) had been sunk and the *Enterprise* badly damaged, the task force was broken up, and we proceeded to Noumea, New Caledonia. We had only been there a short time when we were under way again, headed north for the Solomon Islands. We were in a small group of thirteen ships, consisting of eight destroyers and five cruisers. I did not know it at the time, but I later learned that they were the only ships available to head for Guadalcanal to try to stop Japanese reinforcements from being landed on the island. USS *San Francisco* (CA-38) was the flagship, and I remember that USS *Portland* (CA-33) was also with us, as well as two anti-aircraft cruisers and USS *Helena* (Cl-50). There were also some transports carrying supplies to the Marines on Guadalcanal. We arrived without incident, and the transports unloaded their cargo and left.

On November 12, 1942, our ship was assigned to cruise up the coast and destroy any Japanese barges we found. My battle station was gun director pointer. The gun director, a large 6' X 6' metal box that contained rudimentary computers, was located on the deck directly above the bridge. As pointer, I fired the five-inch guns when we were on automatic fire. Since my gun sight was telescopic, I had an excellent view of the barges. We spent most of the day destroying barges and expending more than half our ammunition. (That would prove to be beneficial later, when there were many fires and explosions on board.) So far, we had not seen any enemy planes or ships, and I heard several shipmates say we probably would be leaving soon and heading back to Noumea. That was how little we knew about what was happening. We were on "four on, four off " watches, and I was scheduled for the mid watch (12:00 to 4:00 am).

Soon after I came on watch, I was looking into my radar scope, and I saw numerous blips on the screen. We were the lead destroyer because we were the only one equipped with radar, which was very new at the time. The ships were in a line, with four destroyers, then five cruisers followed by four more destroyers. I assumed the radar was not working properly, as I was getting blips wherever we trained the antenna. I reported the targets to the gun director officer and told him the radar must be malfunctioning. Then I looked over the top of the director, and, even though it was a dark night, I could see ships everywhere in front of us. About that time, we were told to pick a target and open fire. We trained on a ship, and, since we were on automatic fire, I fired a salvo from the five-inch guns. By that time, we were very close, and when the rounds hit the ship, I could see it was a destroyer. It started burning. We continued to fire and were so close that even the 20-millimeters started firing. In the meantime, the enemy opened fire.

In the first fifteen minutes, we were hit enough times to knock out most of our guns, and we took a hit in the engine room, causing us to lose propulsion; we were dead in the water. There were about six of us on the gun director deck, but the shipmate on the front of the director, Sparky, was still taking ranges and calling them out. I was still firing on the destroyer when we took a direct hit on the face of the gun director, and one salvo went into the bridge. Surprisingly, I found out later that most of the personnel on the director had survived the hit except for Sparky and the gun director officer. (I later learned that the officer had survived.)

I was shaken up but not hurt. The director was now useless, so I started down to the bridge. A fire control striker (an inexperienced sailor) who was also on the director asked me to help him, because his leg was broken. I got down onto the bridge, and he slipped down on my back. I carried him down another deck to the area near the chart house. In the meantime, as enemy ships went by, their guns hit us repeatedly. I could hear our torpedoes being fired, but they did not have time to arm because the enemy ships were so close, so they were all duds. The *Cushing* was still afloat, as most of the damage was above the waterline. The noise, screams, fires and explosions were so loud and confusing that it made me feel as though I was in a very bad nightmare. I kept wondering what it would feel like when I got hit; I soon found out. I put my friend down on the deck, and, as he said he hurt so bad, I was trying to give him a shot of morphine from a small syrette we all carried in our first aid kits. That probably saved my life, because while I was bending over him, a large enemy ship hit us again, but on the starboard side of the charthouse; we were on the port side. The explosion and shrapnel came my way, and I was hit in the left leg and took a piece of metal behind my left ear that knocked me unconscious.

I had a kapok life preserver on, and later I found many small pieces of shrapnel in the jacket. Being bent over, most of the blast had gone over me. When I revived, my friend was still there, but he had additional injuries. He wanted me to continue to help him, but I was unable to and told him I could not. He got upset and told me that, if he died, he would come back and haunt me the rest of my life. That sounds funny now, but I think he was serious. (He did, by the way, get off the ship, as I saw him the next night on Guadalcanal.)

There were many fires, and some of the ready boxes (ammunition) at the gun stations were exploding. I did not see anyone, so I sat down on a piece of the quarterdeck because things were pretty fuzzy. A mess attendant I knew came by, and I asked him what was happening. He said the order had been given to abandon ship, but apparently, I had been unconscious and had not heard the order. Stunned and confused with fires, smoke and fuel oil in the air, I figured I had better get off, as the ship would not last long. I don't recall being scared; in the noise and confusion and with my injuries I told the mess attendant to come with me, but he refused, saying he could not swim. I suppose he did go later, as the deck was so hot a person could hardly stand on it. When I hit the water, I was right next to the side of the ship, and every time I started to paddle away, the ship would roll and draw me back. I got away from the side after swimming hard but then found I was swimming in a large pool of fuel oil that was pouring out of the ship. My first thought was to get out of the oil, because fires were spreading to the water in other areas. The oil got into my eyes, and that caused me a lot of trouble, but I heard later that the oil and frequent explosions were reasons that sharks were not a problem the first night. I was fortunate to have a rubber tourniquet in the first aid kit, and I put it around my left thigh because my leg was bleeding badly. I could not stand on it, so I thought it was broken. I later found out the tendon was severed behind the knee, and the leg would not straighten out. I crawled toward the ladder down to the quarterdeck but found it was blown away, so I went around the front of the chart house and found that the ladder on the starboard side was still there. I was crawling, so I went down headfirst—which was a mistake, because I fell most of the way down. I remember that I lost a shoe in the process, and for some reason that really bothered me.

As I floated away, I looked back at the *Cushing*; she was burning, and the explosions continued. After a short time, I luckily found a small raft with no one in it. I got onto the raft but found that it was upside down and the paddles were underneath the raft. I was able to get two paddles and started to move farther away from the ship, because debris was falling into the water near me. Later, I found three other men in the water.

The four of us were all the raft would hold. We were not too far from Guadalcanal, and we saw some lights on the island, so we headed in that direction. All of us in the raft were injured. I remember that one was an officer, the ship's doctor, and he helped me paddle. The other two were not able to help due to injuries. We were all so covered with oil that I still cannot say who they were.

When dawn came, we saw several rafts ahead of us, a mile or so away. They were mostly *Cushing* survivors. I could only see one ship moving, and I thought that if it was an enemy ship, we were done for. It turned out to be one of our heavy cruisers, and heavy damage to its stern had jammed the rudder. That caused the ship to move in a large circle. As the day got lighter, the cruiser started firing at a ship on the horizon. I was hoping the other ship would not return fire, as we were right in the line of fire. The cruiser (I think it was the *Portland*) finally hit the target, because I saw it smoking. It might have been a transport, because the Japanese were trying to land troops on the island, but it was too far away to tell. About mid-morning, I saw some Higgins boats heading toward us from Guadalcanal. They were manned by Marines from Guadalcanal and had come out looking for survivors. We could see them picking up people, and they finally got to us. Because so many were wounded, they would lower the ramp on the bow of the landing craft and drag in as many as possible, then close the ramp as the water was rushing in. After pumping the water out, they would lower it again and pull in more survivors. We headed back to Guadalcanal and were unloaded near a few shacks that had been set up as an aid station. Someone finally got to me and poured sulfa into the leg wound, then wrapped it up—oil and all. They also bandaged my head, put me on a stretcher, and put the stretcher in a shed with other survivors. That night the Japanese sent some ships back in to shell Henderson Airfield.

We were located between the ships and the airstrip, so all the salvos were going right over us. That was a very uncomfortable situation, especially after all the problems of the previous night.

Quite a few of the survivors in the shed with me were not injured but were very sick from swallowing fuel oil while they had been in the water. The oil seemed to get into their lungs, making it difficult to breath.

A good friend of mine was near me and said he felt as though he was suffocating. I managed to find a corpsman, and he brought a small bottle of oxygen. That helped his breathing, but the oxygen was soon used up. I tried to get another bottle, but there was no more. After several hours, my friend got worse, and he died before morning. There were probably others who did not make it for that same reason. The next morning, there was an air raid, and all of us on stretchers were placed in a field so that we would not all be bunched together. Several shipmates walked by me but did not stop. I did not understand why until I realized I was so covered with oil that none of them recognized me. I finally called to a friend I saw, and he told me that they were making up a roster of survivors. All survivors with injuries that would require more than three months to recover would be sent to a hospital in the States. Those needing under three months to recover would be sent to a hospital in Auckland, New Zealand. I learned later that I was in the group to be sent to New Zealand.

We had to wait for C-47s to be flown in to evacuate us. I was put into a large underground bunker, where they stacked us on shelves in our stretchers. That was a miserable period, because it was very hot, there was little fresh air, and, of course, all the people were either sick or wounded. My biggest problem was not my injuries but my arm, which was about the size of a football from the tetanus shot they had given me. I lost track of time, but in a day or two they told us we were to be evacuated.

I was ready to go, because every night there had been at least one air raid; we all wanted out of that bunker. One evening we were put in an ambulance and taken to the airstrip. As we were being loaded onto the plane, an enemy battery started shelling the airstrip. The plane had to take off to avoid being hit, so we were loaded back into the ambulances, and they headed for a different airstrip. The ride was very rough, and everyone was hurting, so I was glad when we arrived. One fellow in the ambulance was in pretty bad shape. I think he said he had been on the destroyer *Laffey*. I asked him what happened, and he said that when his ship had been sunk, he had not been hurt, but while he was in the water, an enemy destroyer had come through his location at high speed. He said he was directly in its path and could not get out of the way. The destroyer's bow had hit him, and he said he remembered it going completely over him. Luckily, the propellers missed him, and he had come up astern of the destroyer, alive but in pretty bad shape. This time we were loaded onto the hospital plane, and we left immediately, because a red alert was on, and enemy planes were coming in from the north as we headed south. When we were in the air, small bottles of brandy were passed out, just as we had received when we had first come ashore. Several said they did not want any and gave them to me, so, by the time we arrived at Espiritu Santo, I was feeling that things were not so bad after all. I spent several days at Espiritu Santo, then we were put onto USS *Solace*, a hospital ship, and taken to New Zealand, where I remained for about four months. Note: After his release from the hospital, Tom was assigned to the commissioning crew of a PT boat tender. He returned to New Guinea, where he served for a year and a half until the end of the war.

LUCKY, LUCKY, LUCKY
Dusty Ward

I went down to Detroit in 1943 to join the Navy. I saw this sign in front of the recruiter's office: "We want you in the Navy Seabees. We build. We Fight." I decided to join and signed up for four years or the duration, whichever came first.

I had to talk my parents into signing for me because I was only 17 years old. I went to five camps in the U.S., always trained by the Marines. I have never figured out why they call them the Navy Seabees and not the Marine Seabees.

We left California and eventually hooked up with the 4th Marine Division in Hawaii. We departed Hawaii by ship around February 1, 1945 and headed for the invasion of Iwo Jima. Because of secrecy, we did not know the destination until we were ready for the landing. We got to Iwo Jima on February 19, 1945, climbed down rope nets to get into LSTs (Landing Ship Troops) each of which held 30 troops, to go ashore.

The LSTs were about 50 feet apart as we hit the shore, landing in the second wave. This was the wave the enemy decided to unload on. They hit an LST 50 feet from ours as we landed. It killed or wounded over half the Marines onboard before they even got to touch land. That was my first of three experiences where I was lucky not to get hit during my first 20 hours on Iwo.

My second close call came when four of us volunteered to carry wounded men from inland to the beach hospital ship. We started at 7 p.m. and carried about 30 men before we finished about 3:30 a.m. All night, we could hear artillery shells going off in the distance. During the night, our outfit moved down the beach 500 yards. We found out later that morning that many of those shells were landing on them, causing heavy casualties. Luck number two, by volunteering and being separated from our outfit, had saved our lives. We later received a commendation for volunteering and carrying the wounded.

Lucky event number three came the next morning, as we reported back to our outfit. I was designated to report to our officers and tell them why we were absent during the night. I went inland and up the hill, introduced myself to the two Marine officers, and told them what happened the night before. It took me about one and a-half minutes to tell them, then they thanked me and excused me. I headed back down the hill towards the water. I got about 50 feet, or approximately five seconds away, when an artillery shell landed where the three of us had just been standing. The two Marine officers were killed as quick as you can snap your fingers. It blew me 75 feet towards the water, headfirst into the fox hole that my buddies had dug. I came up with my hand bleeding, but it wasn't serious enough to go to first aid station. We carried our own first aid kit, so my buddies just patched me up.

Thousands of times since then, I've thought of how lucky I was in those three instances.

After that, we stayed on Iwo. I ran a D-8 bulldozer to help repair the damage done by shelling and bombing. We had to get the airstrip in shape for B-29s coming back from raids on Japan when they couldn't make it to Saipan or Guam. They say our work saved more lives than Iwo Jima cost us.

We stayed on Iwo Jima until December 1, then headed back to the USA with a stop on Guam. We arrived at Seattle December 14, 1945. I made it home, walking in the door at 7 p.m. on Christmas Eve. My mother always said I was the best Christmas present she ever got. She will truly never know all the facts about how I was lucky enough to get there. Because of my volunteering to carry wounded I've done a lot of volunteering in my civilian life as well, accomplishing some great results. So, war, in spite of the loss of life and pain, does bring out some good things.

SAM ABRAHAM[1]
J. Randall Davis

Back in 1914, Dan Abraham perceived Russia as the most antisemitic country in Europe. When World War I broke out and Russia aligned itself with the Allied Powers, Dan, a Jew, joined the Central Powers' Austro-Hungarian army. After the war ended, one of that epic struggle's losers, Austria-Hungary, was dissolved, with part of it becoming the nation of Romania. According to Sam Abraham, one of Dan Abraham's two sons and the primary source of the information included in this narrative, Romanians were even more anti-Semitic than Russians. Consequently, Dan and his wife Rachel emigrated from Romania to the United States in 1923.

Upon arrival, Dan and Rachel Abraham moved into a first-floor apartment in Brooklyn, New York. Directly above them on the second floor lived Rachel's sister, Rachel's sister's husband, and their five children. Directly across the street resided Dan's brother, Dan's brother's wife, and their eight children. In short order, Dan and Rachel expanded the extended family by two, with the birth of their sons: Eli, with whom Rachel had been pregnant while aboard the ship she and Dan took from Europe to America; and, in 1924, Sam.

During Sam's youth, his father taught him about political philosophy, and in particular, Marxism and socialism, two doctrines to which Dan, and consequently Sam, subscribed. The father and son's political sympathies changed in 1939, when Joseph Stalin entered into a non-aggression pact with Adolf Hitler. As a result, for Dan, Sam, and many others, World War II became "the fight for freedom." Sam and his best friend Jim joined the United Sates Army together. Sam recalled that they were promised they would be members of the cavalry and

---

[1] The following is based on an interview conducted by J. Randall Davis in April of 2010, as part of an assignment Mr. Davis completed while enrolled in USC's Master of Social Work program. Per that assignment's instructions, the names of the interviewee and all those he referred to during the interview have been changed.

sleep in the same barracks. As it turned out, they never saw a horse, and while Sam was a combatant in Europe, Jim fought in the Pacific Theater.

Sam's role as a soldier in the campaign against Germany was that of a forward observer, which meant that he functioned as a sort of point man, whose specific task was to report the location of enemy targets to the Allied artillery behind the front line; in effect, he served as the howitzers' eyes. Although Sam performed this duty laudably, he remembered himself as an unhappy warrior, who took his marching orders reluctantly:

The World War II veterans are so old [that the war experience] doesn't seem bad anymore. Everybody's, "Oh, I love the army. Oh, I'm a Marine." Bullshit! Everybody's on your ass. . . . Everybody's forcing you around or shoving you in a place you don't want to be. You ask yourself, "Why are the son of a bitches putting me here?" You feel everybody is trying to kill you.

While Sam, of course, was not killed, he did take some shrapnel in his leg; the resultant infection led to his hospitalization, at which point his experience dramatically changed: "All of a sudden everybody is trying to save me. Everybody! My God, it's so different!" Sam reported that in the end he was awarded 100% disability, and that his experience with the Department of Veterans Affairs over the subsequent years had been uniformly positive. By contrast, Sam reported that it was during his enlistment in the Army that he first encountered anti-Semitism, when a fellow soldier called him "Christ killer." Moments later in the interview, Sam quipped that his stint in the army also marked "the first time I met a Republican." An amusing line, but humor can also serve as a defense mechanism. In this case, it served to deflect the interviewer from the potentially sensitive subject Sam had just broached, prejudice. Sam deftly dodged the topic twice more later in the interview. While Sam was quite aware of the history of anti-Semitism in the 20th century, he did not dwell upon his personal experience of it.

Perhaps Sam's reticence regarding this subject is owed partially to the fact that during World War II he witnessed some of the human suffering wrought by the Holocaust. As a member of the force that liberated Dachau, he saw the emaciated, bedraggled inmates in that concentration camp with his own eyes. Sam also saw firsthand countless casualties of battle. One of his responsibilities as a forward observer was to assess the damage done by allied munitions following an artillery strike. This resulted in his coming upon many dead bodies. He characterized himself during his time on the front as "a piece of junk," by which he meant that he had become completely numb to his milieu: "It did not affect me until after [the war had ended], when I was able to breathe." Given the carnage to which Sam was exposed, his inability or unwillingness to respond emotionally to it may have constituted fundamentally healthy coping on his part. Such numbness is commonplace amongst those deployed in kill zones; it represents a defense mechanism seemingly instinctively defaulted to by combatants, an adaptation whose purpose is the protection of those combatants' minds.

Sam possessed another motive for "making his mind blank and not wanting to know about anything"—in particular, about anything regarding the United States military's placement of its cannons behind the front line. Sam had been told that the adversary put a premium on the capture of forward observers like him, as the foe believed forward observers would know the allied artillery's location. Thus, Sam feared that if he were taken prisoner, he might well be tortured by his captors in order to extract information from him. The fact that he was a Jew exacerbated Sam's fear; he dreaded what the Germans might do to a Jewish prisoner. For that reason, when on duty as a forward observer, Sam did not keep his dog tags on his person, because inscribed on those tags was the telltale "H" for Hebrew.

Sam's role as a soldier in the campaign against Germany was that of a forward observer, which meant that he functioned as a sort of point man, whose specific task was to report the location of enemy targets to the Allied artillery behind the front line; in effect, he served as the howitzers' eyes. Although Sam performed this duty laudably, he remembered himself as an unhappy warrior, who took his marching orders reluctantly. Sam stated, "The [World War II] veterans are so old [that the war experience] doesn't seem bad [anymore]. Everybody's, 'Oh, I love the army. Oh, I'm a Marine.' Bullshit! Everybody's on your ass. . . . Everybody's forcing you around or shoving you in a place you don't want to be. [You ask yourself,] 'Why are the son of a bitches putting me here?' You feel everybody is trying to kill you." While Sam, of course, was not killed, he did take some shrapnel in his leg; the resultant infection led to his hospitalization, at which point his experience dramatically changed. He recalled with amusement, "All of a sudden everybody is trying to save me. Everybody! My God, it's so different!" Sam reported that in the end he was awarded 100% disability, and that his experience with the Department of Veterans Affairs over the subsequent years had been uniformly positive.

Sam's precautionary measures attested to his especially fit instinct for survival, which was celebrated by his fellow forward observers, witness their adage, "Leave it to Sam." As forward observers, they were often required to move into unknown, and potentially dangerous, territory ahead of the force behind them. Fortunately, Sam had an extraordinary knack for formulating an escape plan as the forward observers advanced; specifically, he possessed an uncanny ability to spot a route via which they could make a hasty exit, if need be. Sam's talent was considered invaluable by his peers, for if the enemy opened fire, they had to retreat rapidly, and not by the same path they had taken in, which by that time was likely targeted by the opposing side. The fact that Sam, and perhaps some of his comrades, survived World War II owed in part to his quite remarkable capacity to adapt to his environment. He was a reluctant, but very competent, soldier.

NINE DAYS AT IWO

Ray Resler

USS *LST-792*, which measured 328 feet long by 50 feet at the beam, was built in Pittsburgh, Pennsylvania, in the summer of 1944. Our crew sailed her down the Ohio and Mississippi Rivers to New Orleans, where she was commissioned on October 2, 1944. The ship transited the Panama Canal and stopped in San Diego en route to Pearl Harbor. While at Pearl Harbor, combat troops and cargo were loaded onto the LST (Landing Ship, Tank). We continued to the islands of Eniwetok and Kwajalein, arriving in Saipan on February 10, 1945; then we sailed for Iwo Jima. Our top speed was 11.6 knots.

Our ship was about 18 miles off Iwo Jima on D-Day minus one. We had sailed about 700 miles from Saipan, along with a convoy of 35 other vessels. With a crew of 100 U. S. Coast Guard personnel, *LST-792*, captained by LT Charles M. Garrett, carried 360 Marines (elements of the Fourth Marine Division) along with 40 Army soldiers and Navy Seabees. Our cargo was about 500 tons of tanks, trucks, jeeps, and other equipment and supplies.

On that Sunday morning, Army Chaplain James Coffee held church services on the vehicle ramp at the forward part of the ship. He leaned against the dogging chains (which secure the ship's crane on the vehicle ramp) to steady himself against the ship's roll. His hair and papers were blowing in the brisk wind as he addressed the 50 or 60 men in attendance. Later that afternoon, the chaplain baptized Sailor Lawrence Turnquist in a water-filled cavity between the bow doors and the vehicle ramp. The seventeen-year-old n'erdo-well was evidently anticipating the next day's invasion with newly found piety.

The troops on board passed the afternoon topside by shooting craps, playing poker, telling stories, writing letters, or just lying out in the sun. The decks below were segregated, with separate facilities for black and white personnel. The gunners and I stood gangway watches dressed in whites, each armed with a .45 caliber pistol.

Iwo Jima had three Japanese airstrips that were the source of costly enemy raids on our bases in the Mariana Islands. We learned that the objectives of the coming invasion were to capture the airstrips and the enemy's observation post and fort at Mt. Suribachi and then to occupy the island.

As the afternoon wore on, the combat troops on board received their ammunition—60 rounds each for carbines and M1s—and their food rations. The men did not want excess weight in their packs and were trading or giving away their personal gear for cigarettes, candy, soap, and the like.

D-Day was Monday, February 19, 1945. Reveille for all hands on LST-792 was at 0400 hours. I was a Fire Controlman, Second Class, and my job, as the ship's "recognition expert," was to identify incoming enemy planes and input their ranges. From our offshore position, I could see the island clearly, with Mt. Suribachi, an old volcano some 550 feet high, on the southern end. Through powerful binoculars, I could also see the first combat troops land at Yellow Beach #2.

All around were different types of vessels. LST-792 pulled several miles out to sea. Our planes were strafing, dropping bombs, and firing rockets at the island. The Marines that were already on shore were facing an enemy entrenched in pillboxes, bunkers, blockhouses, and machine gun nests, all connected by tunnels.

We were scheduled to be one of the first on the beach, but conditions on the shore were delaying the operations. Loose black volcanic sand and ash covered the island and the beaches. The first vehicles to disembark the landing craft had bogged down and were unable to move inland off the beach. The beach was impassable for the tanks and equipment still on board, and cargo from the vessels was being man-handled.

Our troops on LST-792 were getting anxious as we sat offshore for three more days. At night, the troops were sleeping on and under tables, on shower floors, in jeeps, in trucks, and in machinery on the tank decks. We watched as the hospital ship USS Samaritan arrived between us and the beach. We were looking for nurses on board through our binoculars; then we saw the small boats full of wounded crowding around its gangplank.

The Seabees and Marines on shore were busy rigging steel mesh "roadways" called Marston mats to allow armored tracked vehicles, cats, and dozers to move cargo from the beached vessels. On D-Day+3, ships began to unload vehicles and supplies in quantity.

When D-Day+4 (February 23) dawned, it was raining and cold, and the surf was very high. Around 1000 hours, we could see the American flag atop Mt. Suribachi. On the ship, we were told to stand ready to hit the beach with our men and cargo. After several attempts, we landed on Red Beach #2 near dusk at 1745 hours.

That night, all the ships in the area were making smoke for protective cover. The battle was raging a half-mile away, but the smoke obscured it. Then anti-aircraft guns from the other side of the island opened up, illuminating the sky with tracers. A mortar hit our starboard side; then more mortars blasted our ship. Five men were wounded. At 1900 hours, we had to retreat. Fortunately, our engineer, LTJG John E. Waite, had had the foresight (against orders) to keep one of our ballast tanks full. The 300 tons of water in the tank allowed us enough traction to pull free of the beach. We moved 200 yards out and maneuvered to find anchorage. As we watched, at least eight shells landed in the sand on the exact spot where we had been beached. We had pulled out just in time.

I had spent an uneasy night in my sack, itching from the fine-spun glass insulation material that had landed there when the mortar had blasted a gaping hole in the adjoining starboard bulkhead. On D-Day+7, all the Marines on the ship were ready to go ashore, with packs on their backs and weapons ready. It took most of the day to unload the Marines and the Army equipment. That night, we took a mortar on the port side. We had sustained 13 mortar hits in all.

On D-Day+8, *LST-792* was found seaworthy, and we received orders to return to Saipan for extensive repairs. Our next landing: Okinawa.

SERVICE UNVEILED
Bruce Rowe

I own a baseball, given by a friend of my grandfather, Charles Austin "Buck" Rowe, on the occasion of my father's birth. The friend wrote this message on the baseball, "To Buck Jr. You must start practicing now if you are to be as good as Buck Sr."

Living up to your father's legend is a tough burden to carry through life. Especially when you also carry the same name. That was the way my father, Charles Austin Rowe, Jr. entered life.

His father, Charles Sr., was an athlete and aviation pioneer, now enshrined in the Arizona Aviation Hall of Fame at the Pima Air and Space Museum in Tucson, Arizona. The senior Rowe had an amazing life. Though always humble about it, he surely could have won bragging rights against all but the most famous aviation figures. And many of those figures were counted among his associates and friends, including Howard Hughes, Billy Mitchell, Jimmy Doolittle, William Boeing, and American Airlines founder C.R. Smith.

To further set the highest of bars with which CAR, Jr.'s life would be measured, here's a recap of some of the accomplishments of CAR, Sr.:

Scholarship athlete in football and baseball at Gettysburg College

- Professional baseball player (prior to Navy enlistment)
- Naval Aviator #736, trained in Pensacola, Florida to fly night bombing missions
- World War I combat vet flying bombing missions against German subs and other "targets of opportunity" from airfields in France
- Pilot participating in Mitchell's first tests of bombing ships from the air
- Chief Pilot, Cuban American Airlines
- Supervisor/Aeronautical Inspector, Southwest Region, U.S. Department of Commerce out of Los Angeles International Airport
- Southwest representative for Gulf Oil to the aviation market, 1937-1961, including piloting a company

issued Stinson "Gulf Hawk" later displayed in the Smithsonian National Air and Space Museum

Immediately, living up to the legend became an impossible task for my father. At nine months, he had his first asthma attack. At the same time, the doctor diagnosed phlebitis in his left leg. Further testing revealed numerous allergies. Doctors started him on lifelong prescriptions of Ephedrine and an adrenaline atomizer to ease the symptoms. "Athlete" was not going to be an option for young Charles. Neither was the military as it turned out. Initially classified 1A for the U.S. Army in 1942, the phlebitis soon led to his discharge.

I never talked with my father about his struggles with growing up in the shadows of the legend of his father. Dad was a father in the '50s mold: stoic and not to be questioned. I admit I was intimidated enough to never bring up the subject with him. I just sensed the struggle through his interaction with his dad and an unseen tension between the two. Part of the Greatest Generation, my impression was that he felt some guilt and inadequacy in not serving on the battlefield as so many of his contemporaries had. Though his physical limitations were certainly no fault of his own, it would be only natural for any of us to feel the weight of an implied, unfulfilled legacy.
Recently, I've realized there's another view of my father's life.

Within months of his Army discharge, my dad hired on as a mechanic at Lockheed Aircraft Corp. His assignment was Love Field, Dallas, Texas. During the war, the U.S. Air Force 5th Ferrying Group operated there. Together with a contingent of the Women Air Force Service Pilots (WASP) the mission was to modify and send new Lockheed P-38 Lightning fighters into both the Europe and Pacific theaters.

Rather than ship the planes, at risk to German U-boats, the U.S. military—with consultation all the way up the chain to President Roosevelt—began flying P-38s to the UK. The WASP unit would do the flying.

But the P-38 needed an increase in range to make it work. Lockheed determined it wasn't cost effective to make the alterations on the assembly line, so workers like my dad modified the fighters to carry additional, range-boosting drop tanks of up to 310 gallons of fuel. The connecting pylon that he and his co-workers mounted under the wing on either side of the pilot compartment, could carry two different belly tanks, or bombs for shorter missions.

The smaller tanks of about 165 gallons were in greater supply, and so the mission called "Operation Bolero" began. With fueling stops in Canada and Greenland, nearly 200 of the P-38Fs successfully made the first flights across the Atlantic from July to August 1942. Reaching the U.K., the P-38 became the first USAF fighter ever to be delivered across the Atlantic under its own power.

A Smithsonian Channel documentary series, *Air Warriors*, provides perspective on the war-winning impact of the P-38. Pilots raved about its speed, firepower, and focused design for defeating newly minted German and Japanese bombers. The novel design featured twin booms carrying one engine each and running aft to a dual-rudder tail. The main wing spanning the booms supported a central, short "nacelle" housing the cockpit. It was the first aircraft to break 400 mph, versus typical 250 mph speeds before. And pilots had four .50 caliber guns firing 4,000 rounds per minute, together with a 20mm canon in the nose directly in front of them. The centered position made the aircraft deadly accurate.

The P-38 Lightning was a key component in destroying German supply lines in Europe and Asia, along with devasting German and Japan air forces.

In its most famous mission, P-38s enabled the U.S. to strike a strategic, turning-point blow in the Pacific. Operation Vengeance would track and kill the number one strategic target in the theater, Admiral Yamamoto, the mastermind of the attack on Pearl Harbor. U.S intelligence had broken the code on Japanese communications and knew Yamamoto was aboard one of two bombers flying to an inspection visit at Bougainville, Papua New Guinea.

Only the P-38 had the range to chase down the Japanese bombers without early detection, successfully shooting down both. Yamato crashed to his death on the island.

Think how that mission alone reframes my father's "lack" of service during the war. Along with every military veteran serving in World War II, he was also a cog in the machine that saved the world from an unthinkable fate.

One of my dad's gifts that I witnessed firsthand, was his mechanical aptitude. As boys, my two brothers and I would sit for hours watching him take apart clocks, motors, bicycles, and toys, then figure them out and fix them. As he worked, we watched him draw the same tools from the same toolbox—painted in P-38 Night Fighter black—that he'd used to ready the fighters to win a war. It's certain that this was the ability that he contributed in his service to the country.

Today, my brothers and I can fix damn-near anything, and that's the proud legacy of my dad that lives in us.

Charles Austin Rowe Jr., my father, was one of countless men and women who served during World War II, but who will never be called "veteran." He won't ever live up to the legend of Charles "Buck" Rowe either. But we can all be sure he, and all those men and women, were just as much a part of the Greatest Generation.

A GREAT SURPRISE
Anonymous

What is a great surprise? – An unusual gift, an unplanned visit from a friend, finding a hidden treasure in the sand? It could be anything leaving one with a feeling of euphoria, anything able to lift the spirit. But for me, what constitutes the ultimate level of surprise is an unexpected gift of compassion and humanity – given by one individual to another – especially in extraordinary circumstances. Time has made me into a bit of a skeptic – well maybe more than a bit – as it is often difficult to find the good in people. Man's inhumanity to man never ceases to amaze me, yet an act of kindness always surprises me. Here is my favorite story that gives me some hope.

A plane crash lands in enemy territory at a time in history when the hatred of Americans for the Japanese was at an all-time high, and theirs for us was even more intense. An Army pilot was assigned to fly one of the prisoners from the sight of the crash to another area for internment. Strangely and certainly surprising was the pilot's reaction to this man whom he had been ready to kill only moments before. Instead of loathing and bitterness he had expected to feel, an understanding and sympathy engulfed him. Perhaps it was the similarity of the two – both fighting under orders, both similar in age and rank, and both in the air corps of their country, but whatever the reason, a strong connection and a feeling of empathy developed between them.

As a result, the pilot who was flying the plane that was transferring the downed aviator attempted to establish some communication with his charge. This was difficult because his English was very limited and the other pilot, being a prisoner, was reluctant to speak.

However, it was when the pilot of the transport plane arranged for the prisoner's family pictures, which had been confiscated, to be returned to him that an attempt was made to respond, and some very limited information was exchanged. Their time together was brief, and they soon parted in different directions each man going where destiny took him. During the remainder of the war, and for many years following, the pilot often thought about the prisoner and hoped he would eventually be able to return safely to his family, the ones in the photo that he had returned. In a time of hell, two men met briefly and as enemies; each in the service of his country. Each hating the horror of war and yet, between them a small, fleeting connection was made. If you heard the story I have just related, you would expect it to end here. However, you would be shocked to learn the end of the story. You see, the Japanese flying officer. Lt Ohunuke from the Japanese 1st Air Division was the pilot assigned to fly the American prisoner of War, my brother – from the Kurile Islands to a prison camp in Hokkaido. The year was 1945 and both men were in their early twenties, and for a brief moment in time one human being reached out to another.

How do I know this? Because in September 2003, 58 years after the incident, and through several intermediaries, there was contact between the two men. Through the intervening years, the now Mr. Ohnuki often told the story of the meeting. Eventually, a friend of his made the initial contact after he read some information on the Internet about my brother. He recognized the name and the facts as being the same that he had heard so many times before.

The word surprise is insufficient to convey the excitement when the first e-mail arrived. After all., it was 58 years later, the men were both 83 years old. So, today, when I remember these events, and I recall the compassion of just one civilized individual during a time of extreme hate, even I, the skeptic have some hope for the future.

THE STORY NEVER TOLD
Frank Sutton

Hoping to resurrect valuable shards from mostly banal rubbish, I have been re-reading my dog-eared letters from 1944 and 1945 that my stepmother saved. They reveal the ambivalence and boredom, as well as the impulsiveness and creativity, of a teen-aged service member. Sharing these wartime missives, and the vignettes that I've composed based on them, can be both satisfying and sad.

Three nights ago, I read one correspondence-inspired story to my wife Joan. After finishing it, I hesitated and then surprised myself with these words: "Joan, there's an afternoon in France that I've never written about or repeated to anyone." She waited, just listened . . . and then I told her about it.

It's still not clear to me why this confession comes more easily now. It may be that since I've just finished reading Stephen Ambrose's tome D-Day, I have become more aware of both sides' horrible deeds and mistakes that fateful day. This does not dissipate my regret, but it has helped to explain the denial by me, and thousands like me, of a lot that happened during that awful time.

I clock back to an unusually relaxed, late November afternoon. No enemy contact today, as our platoon is pulled back to a relief and rest area, while other infantry grunts are closer to the front, playing the usual lottery of fate.

My hole is dug and my BR clean. I seal a V-Mail home and open a K-ration. I nibble on the hard cheese, pretending it is roast beef. A stream nearby makes water plentiful, saving my canteen. I indulge in a leisurely "whore's bath," using a sliver of soap and a helmet filled with warm water. Waxed K-boxes are always good kindling.

From out of the woods, to my left, a silent visitor, his red top pecking, wobbles towards me. This must be either a mirage or a hallucination. I spy no feathered harem, but I guess he must have a bevy of giggling girlfriends nearby. I hadn't tasted eggs in months—

since being transported aboard a troopship—and those eggs were powdered. Fantasies of rooster fricassee float before me.

Impulse takes over; I have no plan. I edge away from my hole and tiptoe toward my guest, who is a stone's throw away. Our eyes meet. His upright stare detects neither a prospective lover nor a threat. He has probably co-existed with other two-legged creatures before. Neither one of us moves for a time, and then he returns to his searching for grubs. As my right foot dances slowly towards him, his red notch elevates. Seeing no expected handouts, he quickly retreats.

Not knowing a reassuring poultry aria, I hum softly in faulty French and follow leisurely, hoping to serenade, not startle, my pecking prey. I do not see him eye me, but his DNA radar somehow knows how to maintain a proper distance. All the while, this carefree clucker leads me along unmarked paths, wandering up and down hills, circling trees and hedges.

For forty minutes I patiently track him. Then abruptly, he takes a quick hop and flies, disappearing over a ridge. He knows home is near. I bolt after him, and once I summit the ridge, a tarpaper roof appears. My fine-feathered friend has lit on it and is resting. Then he flutters over the edge and disappears.

Thinking I've lost him to his family, I nevertheless proceed with my quest. I carefully step across the narrow space from the bluff's top down and onto the tarpaper roof. I peek over the rim and see only an old farm's cluttered backyard. I continue watching, waiting, and listening. No birds. Only quiet.

I'm about to admit defeat and retreat, when from below I suddenly hear the sound of a door break open and spouting, angry voices . . . in German! My heart races; my face and armpits weep. A sitting duck, I am scared shitless and can't think clearly. My weapon's back with my gear; no enemies were supposed to be near. I touch the one grenade always clipped to my jacket. I snap it off, pull the pin, wait the eternity of four seconds, and heave it below. I flatten on the roof and hear shrapnel splattering with the blast. I listen. No voices or moans. Thirty hour-like minutes creep by. I hear no movement. Total silence.

I ease myself off the roof and onto the bluff, crawl up the incline, and then run from the scene. It is beginning to darken. I follow my footprints and the bird's scratches in the snow back to my hole and collapse. I don't meet a single one of my fellow soldiers upon my return; I was not missed. I don't tell anyone. I hear no reports of this incident, and two days later, we finally move back to the front.

For sixty-seven years, I've told no one, until I shared it with Joan a few days ago. I have never recorded this happening until now. I have carried this guilt of not ever knowing what happened to those German speakers, or to whom those voices belonged. Were they combatants, or were they civilians? My years of denial say I do not want to know.

Link to YouTube video of Frank reading this story:
https://mail.google.com/mail/u/0/#search/video/FMfcgxwChSGQ
WJcxQHSHflQPhRgcTMQh?projector=1

WOMEN VETERANS' STORIES

THE BLACK MADONNA
Maria Ysela Galvan-Dupree

In 2009 I was in Kosovo, on a mission to work with the California Army National Guard, G9 section Division Staff Level Civil Affairs, as a Medical Service Officer. My unit was the HHC 40th ID, Operation KFOR, 11 Task Force Falcon. My primary responsibility was planning and production of civil affairs related documents while enabling the civil-military operation for the commander.

My section played a significant part in this deployment, providing services to the Albanian and Serbian community, such as the Medical Civil Augmentation Program (MEDCAP) and putting together meetings between the KFOR general and the local mayors in our area of operations. MEDCAP provides medical services for the community, including dental and veterinary care.

KFOR soldiers also make a yearly pilgrimage to the village of Letnica, in Kosovo, to see the Church of the Black Madonna. As soldiers with the California National Guard, many of us have walked alongside the Balkan pilgrims. This trip is more than just what our unit called a "combat tourist visit" to see the sights of Kosovo.

The story of Mother Teresa tells about her receiving her calling at the Church of the Black Madonna. Learning that offered me the opportunity to make a promise I keep to this day. A promise that keeps me moving forward. Now when I see similar saints at other Catholic churches, it feels like she is calling me to move forward...not give up.

When we went outside the wire in Kosovo (out of the base), we would wear what we call "full battle rattle" ACUs (Army Combat Uniform), gear that holds our weapons, water, and multiple live ammo magazines. Because our mission included protecting the church, it was not unusual for the community to see a soldier enter the church carrying a rifle and dressed this way. I can visualize myself now with full uniform and armed with my M9.

When our G9 civil affairs section went to see the Black Madonna, I made a "Manda;" a promise between the Black Madonna, God, and myself that if a favor blessed me, I would return a favor or a sacrifice in their name. Mandas are a way of demonstrating thanks for a blessing one asks for from God and the Saints.

I worked for over 13 years with San Diego County as a mental health clinician. At one point, I worked with dual-diagnosed patients—those with a diagnosis of substance abuse and mental health issues.

Most soldiers in the National Guard have two jobs, one as a civilian and one in the service. My National Guard commitment included 23 years of service, and I knew the ins and outs of deploying and the toll it takes on a soldier. I felt I was more than experienced enough to work with Veterans.

God and the Saint honored their part of the Manda with my safe return from Kosovo.

Next, I applied and was hired by one of several Vet Centers in San Diego that provides services to combat Veterans and victims of military sexual abuse (MST). I would be a readjustment counselor, helping Veterans like those who had deployed with me. Exactly the promise—my Manda—I had made to help other Veterans deal with anxiety disorders and family issues as a result of combat missions. Some of the soldiers in my deployment to Kosovo were upset that the Army was not what they thought it would be. One soldier joined the Army right after 9/11, giving up a college scholarship. Like many others, he lost several battle buddies. Several soldiers had family issues, and we all missed our family and friends back home.

Some refused to enter the church, and some were upset with God. In the military, the saying is, either you find God, or you lose your spirituality. But I was going to be like mother Teresa: also receiving my calling at the Church of the Black Madonna. At least that was my plan. I loved working with my Veterans from the Vet Center. I had several groups too. They included two PTSD groups, a stress and relaxation group, and a women's group. At any time, I had over 80 clients to see, at least once every two weeks.

As with any government agency, the process of paperwork can be all-consuming, and the actual services can get lost in accomplishing that process. But my Vets enjoyed the group and attended individual therapy when they could. I would write notes that included their emotional stories of combat and MST. I made sure the reports included enough information to back up their requests for VA benefits and this they appreciated. I would take whoever came in at any time, even during my lunch hour. In not setting boundaries, this came at a price of overwork for me.

After working with the Vet Center for three years, one of my combat Vets committed suicide one month after his discharge. We had worked on a slow discharge, with several sessions to help him in his aftercare. I was his readjustment counselor for over three years; he was a model patient. He was active in his treatment. He went from sleeping in his car to getting an apartment, even completing his bachelor's degree and finding a job.

At the Vet Center, a veteran's case is not completely closed after his last session. A treatment team meeting is held to review all requirements before the case is closed. He had made progress, but some issues came up, and the coping skills he'd used to make progress in all aspects of his life did not register at that critical moment for him.

I stayed home for several weeks to figure things out, while the Veterans Health Administration reviewed his file.

The VA review outcome was not what I expected. My Vet had started drinking excessively. He kept this well hidden from his psychiatrist and me. He also stopped attending church. I only mention this because I believe, from my experience working with combat Veterans, that resiliency includes spirituality. Not necessarily a religion, but trust in something other than yourself.

The Vet center sent letters and cards from my other Vets asking me to return. I felt I needed to talk to a chaplain. I was scared for the soul of my Vet. I wondered if he would not enter the gates of Heaven.

With my beliefs, the chaplain helped me understand several things. One was that my Vet was not in his right mind at the time of his death, and the pearly gates of Heaven would open for him.

Over the next two years, I had dozens of Vets appreciate my services, but after five years, I felt overworked. Now I needed to work on my health. In school, they teach therapists self-care. At work, they tell you not to take it home. It is not easy to do after several hours of listening to traumas. Traumas that I would never share with others. I didn't want others to hear their stories because of privacy issues, but also because I knew it would disturb them.

I had heard so many stories and worked with so many at risk Vets that I thought that I couldn't help them as I had in previous years. Even my commute had taken a toll on my health. Some days I was driving several hours to and from work. I know that health is a complicated issue; I must take care of my own.

But I was conflicted. Was I breaking my Manda by retiring and not working with combat Veterans?

Today I mostly work online as a coach, and recently I passed my California Board of Behavioral Sciences Law and Ethics test. Several of the soldiers I served with have moved on to civilian jobs, advanced in their military career, or retired and are resting, taking care of their health and family. My goal is to one day have a private practice.

Religion and spirituality are difficult for some to understand. It requires faith. Especially for a soldier, whose faith is tested over and over again. Yes, some days are hard for me, and suicide has gone up in the Veteran population since my Vet died. I struggle to keep that faith alive and as the chaplain so sadly said, "suicide will happen again."

I continue to ask God and the Black Madonna to pour blessings over my family, friends, and particularly over all Veterans, especially my battle buddies and soldiers who I had the great privilege of serving with over my 23 years in the service. And so no, I have not broken my promise and I will continue to pay my Manda.

SO QUICK TO JUDGE
Sarah Noel Wood

Under the black fingernail polish,

all black clothes, and a nervous look,

I see a young girl fighting for attention.

Under the hair loss, surgical scars,

and saddened eyes,

I see a woman fighting her cancer.

Under the tattooed arms on wrinkled skin and veteran's hat,

I see a man covering up his battle wounds.

And I wonder, what they all think when they look at me?

TRANSITION

Sarah Noel Wood

Seated in a canoe gliding across the lake ripples, the water slaps beneath me.

Rocking back and forth, the sun shines in and out of the spaces between the trees and warms my face.

My cheeks soak up the warmth for what seems like hours before the clouds move in.

Droplets of rain start to indent the water and sprinkle a cool mist across my skin. Instead of rowing back to shore, I take in the moment.

Minutes pass and a small puddle appears at my feet. Surveying the surrounding waters and shoreline, I try to estimate how long it will take me to hit land.

My scan stops as a glimpse of something in the distance appears. Suddenly, my heart begins to race, and the rain's mist turns to sweat as the canoe drifts closer to an eerie object.

Panic sets in.

Frantically, my hands grab the oars and row towards what I think is a person.

The canoe abruptly halts next to her. Is it a her? All I can see is hair, really long hair, floating on top of the water.

Rain pours down now and begins to blur my vision.

Leaning over the side of the canoe, my fingertips stretch over the water with my eyes still locked on the long hair.

I reach down to touch her. I lift up the soft, slimy strands of seaweed. SEAWEED?!

My eyes pop wide-open, and I scan my bedroom.

Slowly, my heart settles down, and I take a deep breath to exhale. When will these nightmares stop?

I picked up human remains in a land-locked country, yet my mind drowns in the memories.

THE PLOT OF MY LIFE
Sarah Noel Wood

I will never...

I will never get married and have kids.

I will never marry a military man, and if I do, he won't be divorced, with kids.
I will never own a small dog, especially a high-maintenance, fluffy one.
I will never volunteer and if I do, certainly not for rank-less schools,

South Korea, or General Staff.

I will never like the color pink or think to fill my house with it.
I will never stain my brand-new couch, bounce a check or scratch the paint on my car.
I will never cry in public or see a counselor, and I certainly won't become one!
I will never say "I will never" again!

Unless, of course, I want it to come true.

IS THAT A FISH?
Brenda Fonseca

It was a beautiful fish tank. It was not very big, but we figured it was better than the home our fish Dorothy had had before. The tank was two gallons and came with a battery-powered water filter and built-in, ever-changing lights. The tiny gravel at the bottom of the tank created a lovely landscape of the prettiest pinks and neon greens. My friend Thompson and I had picked out the decorative coral and kelp. The imitation coral was a pastel pink and textured with more detail than you would expect from a discounted ornament. The kelp was a light green, and it flowed under the current of the circulating water. The different colors combined with the soft glowing lights made the tank seem like something out of a dream. Dorothy was a small beta fish that we rescued from the shelves of the local Walmart in Pascagoula, Mississippi. She was gorgeous. Her body was a rich blue and where her sapphire scales met the red flow of her fins, the color had the slightest hints of purple. Her fins were my favorite. They were like long pieces of delicate silk, trailing behind her like the train of a wedding dress. We were in love.

It was easy to fall in love when serving in the Navy, especially when you were attached to a ship. A Navy ship is a special micro-society in which the true nature of man is revealed. I had suspected early on in my enlistment that the military might not be what I wanted to do with the rest of my life. In the aftermath of an incident that ended in Dorothy's being dumped overboard, I knew my days in the Navy were numbered.

Thompson and I had snuck her past the bag check and taken her straight up to our workshop, Shop 2, on the fourth deck up next to the bathroom. We hid her in the shelf under the work bench, behind a wall of empty red toolboxes. While we had not read any rules explicitly prohibiting keeping fish, it was loosely implied a ship was no place for pets. However, we were homesick, and having a fish aboard seemed like one small way to feel at home. We had been on the ship for four months, and we were tired of the mundane, everyday work grind. We felt trapped in the floating vessel of endless hazy grey. Dorothy brought color and beauty to our lives.

One fateful morning, Dorothy was discovered by one of the higher-ups. He was a Master Chief, the highest rank attainable by enlisted folk. Unfortunately, in desperate pursuit of a bathroom, he had stumbled into our side of town. He was a short bald man with shiny blue eyes. He had a bit of grey stubble despite the fact he shaved every morning. He reminded me a lot of a haggard, hungover baby. Shop 2's door was wide open, and I had taken Dorothy out from her hiding spot to reorganize the empty red toolboxes. As Master Chief shot towards the restroom, he stopped dead in his tracks, and his eagle eyes locked on to the fish tank.

"What is that?" he demanded.

"What is what?" I innocently replied.

"That thing on the bench! Is that a fish tank?" he asked, as if he had never seen one before. And he must not have, because he called three other men to the shop to investigate this anomaly. First, he called the Electrical Safety Officer. This man dealt with all things that plugged into any ship outlet. He was an uncomfortably tall man who had developed a permanent hunch from slouching down to avoid hitting ceilings. Using his twenty years of experience, the Electrical Safety Officer began to exam the tank thoroughly, to determine the source of power feeding the lights and water filter. He lifted the tank, in a quest to find the cord, and was thoroughly perplexed by the absence of one. How was this mysterious artifact being powered? After minutes of poking and prodding, he concluded the tank was battery powered. He straightened up and announced the tank was not in violation of any safety rule because it had not illegally been plugged into the ship's grid without proper inspection.

Next, Master Chief summoned my immediate supervisor, Chief, to ask if this was really a fish. Chief was a small man with a disproportionately large head. He had brilliant white teeth, and his mouth was stretched in a perpetual nervous smile. He was an inveterate people-pleaser and hated looking bad. Chief reported promptly to Shop 2.

"Is that a fish?" Master Chief demanded.

Chief walked up to the tank and put his face level to it. He peered into the tank and sought to identify the floating creature swimming placidly in the tank. Chief could not decide if it really was a fish, or if it was simply something that looked like one. There was a correct answer here, and he wanted to get it right. After a few minutes of entranced staring, Chief stood upright and confirmed Master Chief's suspicions.

"That's what I thought," said Master Chief, squinting his eyes and rubbing his hands together. Now that he had a witness to the crime, he needed a judge.

Combat Systems Officer was a man of considerable importance but a rather misleading appearance. He was a native Hawaiian. At first impression, his large build and permanent sunkissed tan gave the impression of a kind islander. However, when he spoke, his sharp, crisp words announced that he meant business. When he at long last made his way to Shop 2, I was surprised to hear him chuckle and say, "I haven't seen this before."

At this point, it was all too much for Chief. He jumped into action. He grabbed the tank and awkwardly maneuvered around the crowded space. "Don't worry, we will take care of this," he said, and gestured to me with his bobble head to follow him outside. I walked out behind him.

Outside, Chief began to fumble with the lid of the tank. "What are you doing?" I asked. Chief mumbled through gritted teeth something about destroying the evidence. I was horrified. I tried to reason with him, telling him I could easily just rehome the fish. We didn't have to get rid of her.

But Chief was like a mad dog, pawing at the lid of the tank, trying to pry it off. "We are getting rid of it," he said. The tone in his voice was enough. There would be no further discussion. The fish had to be disposed of.

"But she will die," I said.

"It's a fish. It will be fine. All fish can swim," explained Chief. He was a good liar, I admit, because if I didn't know freshwater fish can't survive in sea water, I would have believed him. As he struggled with the lid, I announced I would do it. I took the tank from his hands and looked down at Dorothy.

She was swimming calmly, almost hypnotically, oblivious to her fate. I felt a deep sadness for her. She was the only beautiful thing in my life at the time. I had been overwhelmed by my life on the ship and somehow, she was impervious to the insidious nature of the Navy. She wasn't affected by the long working hours or bothered by the terrible food. She didn't mind the working parties or the ten o'clock curfews. She was a beacon of normalcy in a life that I was struggling with, something that reminded me I was still a human being. Every day when I pulled her out from her shelf and fed her, I felt like I was home. It was an essential routine for me at the time, one that I found therapeutic.

I removed the lid and poured the contents over the side. Down went Dorothy, gravel, coral, kelp, and all, becoming a miniscule drop in the vast sea. Chief seemed satisfied with the results and turned away to head back inside the ship and do some damage control with the higher-ups. I stared out in the water. I didn't understand. I had given so much to the ship. I had left my one-year-old son and my beloved husband. I traveled to Pascagoula, Mississippi, the armpit of America, to live on a ship that was still in the industrial yards being built. The berthing I slept in often flooded, and the air conditioning was intermittent. There weren't any washers and dryers on the ship, so I had to wear the same uniform for a week straight until the laundry services returned my second pair and rotated them out. On top of my regular duties, every three days, I stood two five-hour security watches with twenty pounds of gear. I was tired, sunburnt, and overworked, and all I wanted, the only thing I wanted in return, was to keep my fish. That was it. It seemed like a fair deal.

However, it makes sense now. The military is not a fair place. You don't get to ask for anything in return. You give everything you can give, and you ask for nothing. I returned to Shop 2 and found Master Chief was the last one still there. He said he planned to petition the Commanding Officer to write a new rule clarifying what personal items were allowed on the ship. The fish incident opened up a new world of paperwork for him, and he walked away excited about his new venture.

I breathed a deep sigh and decided that in order to decompress I would go trim the illegal bonsai tree I kept hidden outside.

INVISIBLE WOUNDS

DON'T JUDGE: MY WOUNDS ARE INVISIBLE AND REAL

Dr. Vernita Black

"The writings reflect our spiritual break-through while serving in the military. May the stories of our challenges inspire you to pay attention to your own invisible wounds."
Anxiety, depression, fear and other psychological issues play an important role in the invisible wounds. It can easily be misinterpreted when they are not seen with the naked eye.

Dr. Vernita Black, Author: The Invisible Wounds of Stress: Inside and Out.

I enlisted in the military in 1981 and served 21 years, both in the Air Force Reserves and active duty in the United States Navy. Traveling and serving my country was important to me. I was healthy and strong, both mentally and physically; eager and ready to see the world. I was all in and no one could stop me from obtaining my goal.

In approximately 1994, after my first deployment, I was one of the first wave of females to be stationed aboard a combat ship, a Spruance-class destroyer. We deployed to the Western Pacific, Indian Ocean, and Persian Gulf. My job as an Interior Communication Electrician was interesting and scary all at the same time.

I remember stepping onboard for the very first time and all eyes immediately shifted directly to me. Everyone stopped to look as if they had seen an alien from outer space. No one wanted to help me with my check-in process. I was pushed aside by many people onboard the ship that day. Several hours went by before I saw my supervisor. After meeting with my department staff, it was apparent that they were reluctant to help. It was as if they were afraid that something bad would happen if they reached out to assist me.

Finally, I headed to the engineer's office to meet the rest of my department—all 20 were men. I was shocked that I did not see any females present. I thought maybe they were out working or doing something else that day. Later, I realized that I was one of the first females to be stationed in that engineering department. I became fearful that I had made a wrong choice. I felt judged for having the nerve to step foot on a military vessel. And not to mention going into the male-dominated field of engineering. What was I thinking? I felt like I'd made the biggest mistake of my life.

I had only been on board for about five minutes and I was being judged without saying a word. It was a different world than I was accustomed to. Everything seemed fast pace and confusing. I couldn't keep up with what was going on. One minute they were in front of me and then seconds later they were gone and back again. This was all so confusing to me. No one communicated or introduced themselves. They practically ignored me.

It was too much and I was ready to leave and go home. I no longer wanted to be a part of that rat race. I was scared. I started getting sick to my stomach and nervous that I was going to pass out. My fears became so intense I froze and could not move. I was terrified by what I was seeing, I thought I was being swallowed by some kind of giant force.

I oscillated between some extreme fear and having some confidence. It was like I was in a battle with myself. Finally, I snapped out of it somewhat and continued to move forward with my check-in. However, I wasn't cleared from all the confusion. My turmoil went on for days and even months as I tried to get out of my fearful, negative thinking. I had to conquer it once and for all. As I continued to let go of the fears, judgments, and pain, I was constantly being ridiculed and judged.

I lived through two decades of my military career facing fears and judgments that had hindered or interfered with my ability to live a positive and productive life in the military. I was tired of being judged! Later, I was stationed onboard a Nimitz-class, nuclear-powered aircraft carrier on the beautiful island of Coronado, California. It was an enormous ship; the beam support (width at the water line) of the ship was approximately 250 feet, the length three times as long as the destroyer. It took a while to learn where everything was on that carrier. It was like a traveling city.

I thought maybe this duty station would be different from the previous ships. Considering it had been almost two decades since women were first stationed aboard military ships, I assumed that everything would turn out just fine. Perhaps, maybe this command would be more accommodating to females. I was hopeful, positive, and proud to be a part of this new duty station. I decided to start new and refreshed. I was again eager and ready to put my best effort forward to be a team player.

I checked-in onboard with a positive attitude; willing, able, and ready to serve. I was somewhat excited about my new endeavors. The ship was scheduled to go on a Western Pacific Deployment. Everyone seemed so focused, excited, and ready to set sail.

After being onboard for several weeks, I started experiencing some negative situations again with many of the men aboard the ship. I tried to push it aside, but once again the judgments and unwelcoming attitude started coming towards me. I tried to maintain my composure while focusing on positive things, but that lasted only a short while.

I started experiencing pain in my stomach that made it hard to perform my daily tasks. The pain was excruciating and intense every day. However, I kept working as I wanted to be a big part of the team and pull my own weight. Initially, I didn't say anything, because I was scared that I would not be believed, that I might be ridiculed, judged, or worse, that I would be deemed a "troublemaker."

The unbearable pain continued, and I knew I had to do something. After several weeks, I decided to reach out for help. I walked into the ship's hospital— what we called "Sick Call" back then— requesting medical attention. The medical assistants and doctors asked me a series of questions, firmly pressed on my stomach in several places, examined me from head to toe, and subscribed Motrin for the pain.

Subsequently, I re-visited the ship's medical clinic for the same pain in my stomach. This time, the pain was worse and it had radiated to my back. The doctors repeated the same examination.

But the pain continued to get worse so I requested to go to the Naval hospital on base. Right away, I was judged and shamed by my entire division for not being a team player. Finally, permission was granted for me to go to the hospital. Once again, all eyes were on me, as if I had committed a crime or betrayed my command by requesting medical care. **The alien appeared again.**

As I entered the hospital, I glanced at my paperwork and was stunned by what I saw. My supervisor had recommended a *psychological* evaluation instead of a physical evaluation. I was enraged.

Fortunately, the evaluation was brief and straightforward. The psychological team noted that I needed a physical evaluation immediately.

When I returned to my command to check-off the ship for testing, the judgment was worse than ever. It was so bad that I had to be medically assisted to the hospital. I never returned to the ship.

Further medical testing discovered a series of tumors that had attacked my pancreas. I became very ill. Over half of my major organs were either removed or re-routed or partially restructured.

I was in deep medical disarray. I had three major surgeries in my stomach along with a total of seven surgeries throughout my military career. My overall recovery took about one year and to this day I am suffering from chronic pain and other medical problems.

When in the military, my surgeries left wounds that can only be seen with an X-ray or scanner. They are invisible except to medical professionals. When I began to realize how my pain had affected me, I wondered why my command or other people could not see my condition in the same way.

And then I got it. I saw and felt my pain, and I could feel and visualize the impact it had on me. But no one else could feel it or understand. Unless you experienced it for yourself you would not be able to know what it's like. Judgments hurt and, as I found, could potentially kill you.

My pain is real, both inside and out. The stressors in my military life contributed to my pain while serving. To be wounded on the inside might be hard to comprehend by those who believe that wounds have to be seen to be real.

Today, my pain is still fresh and real. The judgments of

others in the military did not make the wounds any less so. The stress and anxiety are also as real. I never thought my world might change so drastically.

Now despite the wounds, I can see a shift to a more positive situation. Think before you judge. It can cost a person's life.

* * *

Don't Judge. My Wounds are Real.

Don't judge me for the pain I've endured—my wounds are real though invisible.

Don't judge me for what you can't see with the naked eye—my wounds are invisible.

Don't judge me for scars, cuts, bruises and sadness inside—my wounds are invisible.

Don't judge me for walking too slow—my wounds are invisible.

Don't judge me for not saying my every move—my wounds are invisible.

Don't judge me for being intelligent—my wounds are invisible.

Don't judge me for being absent—my wounds are real, but invisible.

Don't judge me for serving my country—my wounds are real.

Don't judge me for being me—my wounds are invisible.

THE INVISIBLE WOUND
Luz Helena (Stacey) Thompson

"Don't judge a book by its cover and remember, not all wounds are visible. There are a number of invisible wounds that veterans often experience including but not limited to; chronic pain, depression, anxiety, combat trauma, Post Traumatic-Stress-Disorder (PTSD), Military Sexual Trauma (MST), Traumatic Brain Injury (TBI) and more. It is hard to understand that which we cannot see. Creative Writing is just one of the ways we have chosen to share our stories and experiences with invisible wounds. The reality and the recovery."

I did not want to watch television or talk to anyone in the barracks. I put on my headphones and listened to music until I fell asleep. By Saturday afternoon on December 11, 1999, I had made the decision to call my boyfriend, who had recently left the island, before I called my parents and told them what had happened to me. That was before the era of everyone having a personal cell phone. I had a calling card with approximately twenty dollars' worth of minutes on it. I went into the lounge where there was a television and a few couches, thankful that there were no other Marines in the room for the moment. Living in the barracks, one understood that privacy was a luxury, not a right. I knew I did not have much time to tell him every detail before someone was bound to walk in and see me sobbing on the phone. There is no easy way to have a conversation about rape with anyone, especially with no real privacy in a barracks lounge.

"Hello," he said.

"Hey, (long pause) it's me," I said in a whispering tone.

"Hey darling, how are you? I miss you so much. Wish I was there with you. What's going on," he said, curious as to why something seemed different about my voice.

I began to cry, and once the tears started dripping down my cheek, I knew all hell was about to break loose from the inside out.

"What's wrong, darling? What happened," he kept repeating.

I could barely keep it together at that point, and the thought of having to tell him this over the phone made it even more painful. I knew I did not have much time left on my calling card, so I took a breath and said, "I went out Thursday night with a few Marines, and I'm pretty sure I was drugged with something, but I do not know what. I keep having flashes, and I do not remember everything, but I know what he did to me. Oh, my God! How the fuck did this happen?"

I broke at that moment. I did not say anything after that sentence, because I could not. Snot was dripping from my nose, and I was not just crying—I was weeping over the phone—the kind of crying that leads to hyperventilating and renders you literally unable to speak. He stayed on the phone with me and listened to me cry, as I sat in the chair curled up in a ball with my head in my hands and the phone pressed against my ear.

He told me, "You have to breathe. Where are you? Are you safe? Please breathe, darling. Please just tell me you're okay?"

"I'm okay," I said. Between each breath, I was able to mutter the words, "I'm okay. I'm in the barracks." Once I calmed down a bit, I told him, "I was raped by my sergeant. He took me out of a nightclub, and I barely remember much, but I know what happened. I remember all the flashes and the blanket and--" I broke down again and could not say much more. I must have sounded hysterical to him and not in a funny kind of way at all.

He said, "You have to report it to someone. Tell someone what happened."

"I did," I said in between breaths. "I already did. She's taking care of it".

"Who is taking care of it?" he asked.

"My female sergeant. I told her what happened, and she said to go back to the barracks and that she'd take care of it".

I was starting to get angry because I could not say what I wanted to. The emotions I had during that phone call overtook my ability to articulate myself. I did not want to discuss any more of the details, even though he was not concerned with details at that moment.

He said, "You know this is not your fault, right?"

I said, "Yeah, I know," but I did not truly know that. I blamed myself for not being able to protect myself. I was a Marine, sworn to protect others, but what kind of Marine was I if I could not even protect myself from being raped? Those are the sick kind of thoughts one has following the devastating trauma of sexual assault in the military.

He asked, "Did you call your parents yet?", and I told him I had not.

"I wanted to talk to you first. I'm not ready to call them yet, and I'm not even sure how to tell them. What do I do now? I'm so fucking scared, and my throat and body hurt so bad." I had been forced to perform oral sex prior to the rape, and the terrifying feeling of someone forcing you to perform a sex act is something that never leaves your mind.

My boyfriend told me over the phone to go back to my room and get some sleep. He reassured me that my female sergeant was probably handling business right now and that I should not worry, because at least I had told someone. He said, "Let her handle this. She's a sergeant, and she'll know what to do. Just take care of yourself this weekend and call me back tomorrow. Promise you'll call me back."

"I promise I will. I love you." I hung up the phone and went back to my barracks room, hoping not to pass anyone in the hallway leading up to my room. After talking to him, I was emotionally exhausted. I had been crying for hours and craving the comfort of sleep once again, but that was the night I had my first nightmare about the rape. It was terrifying, and I remember waking up sweating and in a panic. I could barely get back to sleep and was too frightened to leave my bed. I lay there in the dark until I could not handle it anymore. I got up and turned on the lights in the bathroom. I let the shower run and sat on the bathroom floor, crying. My roommate tried to comfort me, but all I wanted was to be left alone. I did not want anyone to see me like that. I was ashamed of not being able to maintain any sense of bearing or self-control over my emotions. The Marine Corps taught us how to compartmentalize and reminded us of the importance of not losing one's shit in public. Yet here I was, coming apart at the seams, completely untrained and unprepared to handle the level of trauma I had just experienced.

When I woke up on Sunday morning, I had difficulty breathing without pain, and there was a burning feeling in the back of my throat. I knew where it came from; the details of that night still haunted me. The pain was bad enough that I needed to see a doctor. My roommate escorted me to the naval hospital on base, and I remember being thankful for her company. I did not want to be alone with a male Navy doctor or nurse in the room, especially after having been raped. She watched over me that weekend and did not leave my side, but she did not tell anyone what had happened either. I do not blame her for that. We were both scared, but I knew I had done the right thing by reporting it to my female sergeant, and she had said she would "take care of it."

I made the decision again in the hospital that it did not need to be reported. As a female Marine, I did not want to undermine my female sergeant and tell someone else, which might insinuate that I did not trust her ability to handle the situation. I also worried that I would get in trouble if I reported it again to someone in the hospital and stepped outside both my chain of command and my branch of service. In the military, you do not mess with the chain of command—you respect it, and when you are told to do something, you do it. When your sergeant tells you that she will take care of something like this— something this big— you trust her. You are taught to trust your fellow Marines at times like this. We were a family—but I had just been raped by a brother in the service. Those were the thoughts of a scared nineteen-year-old Marine with only sixteen months' experience in the Corps.

The effect that reporting the rape might have on my career was a concern of mine; I thought back to when I had reported sexual harassment just months earlier. I was made to feel ashamed of ever reporting the harassment. I was transferred to a new unit after reporting the incident, and no punishment came to the Marine who did it. I worried about how many people would eventually find out, because I had learned the hard way that information like that always spread like wildfire throughout a unit. I will never forget how I was treated by other Marines after I reported sexual harassment in my previous unit. I felt a tremendous amount of shame, simply because reporting rape or any sexual assault or harassment was frowned upon.

In 1999, there was no support, advocacy, or privacy for those of us who experienced such treatment while in service. I suppose it is safe to say that, during the time I spent in the military, I learned that sexual harassment was viewed as nothing more than an occupational hazard, to which women had to adapt and overcome their objections. Essentially, one could suggest that, as Marines, we were expected to "suck it up" and not be so sensitive. As female Marines, we were expected to remain professional—always. Crying to your boss because someone grabbed your ass or made a sexual innuendo toward you in the office suggested weakness on your part. Tattletailing every time you did not like what the boys were saying to you or how they were "eye-fucking" you, as we called it, suggested a lack of strength in one's character. Dammit, we were Marines, not a bunch of Girl Scouts. I learned the first time I reported sexual harassment that I was viewed as "the problem" for causing trouble in the unit by making such allegations. The action of a grown man sexually abusing his position of power over me as a Staff Non-Commissioned Officer in the United States Marine Corps was not the issue then; I was. But rape, in my mind, was serious shit, and therefore I did not regret telling Sgt. Anderson what had happened. I just did not want anyone else to know. I knew that, despite the crude remarks people might make about me, it had to be reported.

In the hospital, I kept quiet, and so did my roommate. I had already told Sgt. Anderson everything I could remember. In the Marines, we had an unspoken understanding of the metaphoric totem poles wrapped in red tape, and we knew where we stood on those totem poles according to our rank. We understood that there are certain things you do not do in the Marine Corps—and ignoring the chain of command is one of them. I did not mention the rape to anyone at the hospital. I took the medication I was prescribed (Tylenol with codeine in liquid form) and went back to my barracks room with my roommate as instructed. I was put on bed rest for four days and told to report back to my unit the following Thursday for work. Sgt. Anderson never once came to the barracks to check on me that weekend or in the days to follow. I did not see her again until I returned to the office, believing that she would have taken care of the issue by then.

* * *

Seven months had passed since the rape, and it was July of 2000. I had only been back in the U.S. for about a week. I had done everything I could to simply survive in Okinawa for six months following the rape before the Marine Corps had decided to separate me with an Other Than Honorable (OTH) discharge. I had thought about suicide daily, especially after I had come to realize that my separation from the military was nothing short of retaliation for reporting rape.

I awoke in the guest room of my parents' house, and a disabling feeling of defeat came over me. I knew that I could not continue waking up in that house anymore—at least not with the frightening thoughts that were trapped in my head. I did not want to let anyone see the pain I was in or the daily crying spells that felt uncontrollable and excessive. I did not want anyone to hear me when I woke up screaming and in a panic or to see me curled up into the fetal position at the corner of my bed, shaking in fear— that involuntary shaking that happens when the body has just been pumped with adrenaline from the images of nightmares.

I had lived what felt like a lifetime in just two short years, and now I was right back in the same sad place where I had started. I thought about suicide a lot, but I never fully surrendered to the dark thoughts of ending my life. My grandmother, whom I loved dearly, was still alive, and I knew it would destroy her if I took my life. I knew I could not do that to her. I had made it home safely to a place where no one from the military could hurt me anymore. The problem was that no one knew how to help me either. I was not afforded any mental health care from the military as a result of the character of my discharge. Getting an OTH was almost as bad as a dishonorable discharge, and it stripped me completely of all my veteran benefits. I had no access to support from the Department of Veterans Affairs, because I was no longer viewed as a veteran. My service in the military no longer seemed to matter. I was completely cut off from all communication with anyone in my previous unit, and I had absolutely no one to guide me through the transitional phase of leaving the military and returning to civilian life. I was left to care for myself in complete isolation from the institution I had once called my family.

My parents did not understand the scope of what had happened to me, and, to be honest, I do not think anyone wanted to understand it. To understand the rape, the betrayal, and the impact of the six months I had remained in Okinawa following the rape, we would have had to process it together as a family. To process it, we would have had to talk about it, and my family avoided sensitive topics at all costs. They dealt with my rape in the same way they had dealt with my adoption earlier in my childhood; we did not talk about it. What I experienced during my military service was not the purple elephant in the room; I was the purple elephant. The "let bygones be bygones; you are lucky you even made it back from Okinawa" attitude became the way we dealt with it. Looking back, I understand that my parents were scared. They too had been traumatized by what had happened to me, and they did not know how to deal with all that had transpired, so they did not deal with it. It was put to the side with all the other taboo things my family did not like to discuss.

I do not know why I had the expectation that talking with my mother about rape was going to be different than talking about my adoption. My mother never once spoke to me about her feelings regarding the miscarriage of a child before deciding to adopt. I never knew the details of her story, and I find it incredulous, in retrospect, that I imagined she would be willing to discuss the intimate details of my life. My experience with my mother while growing up suggested to me that she was a very private woman who kept her thoughts and feelings to herself about her life before she had children. I tried to do what I had been instructed to do by my parents and to let the rape slip into the past. I was fresh out of the Marines, and my mind was still programmed to follow orders and do what I was told. I tried to let bygones be bygones. I locked away my feelings somewhere in the dark, bottomless pit of my mind, but the feelings kept creeping back out. I had memories and flashes of images I tried to push away. I tried so hard to make the memories stop, but they would not. Writing was all I could do to try to ease the pain of everything I had experienced.

My nightmares were becoming a lot more frequent, and it was time for me to get away before anyone knew just how deep down the rabbit hole I had fallen. I needed to get away and isolate before anyone in my family knew what was happening to me. I found a small, one-bedroom, basement apartment to rent, not far from my parents' house. I needed a place to shed my tears privately because I knew no one in my family was equipped to handle the reality of my rape and the pain I was in. I was desperate to seclude myself, because I was worried that, if I did not begin to detach, someone would notice that I was losing my mind. I was terrified that, if anyone knew what I was going through, they would lock me up in a psychiatric ward—and rightfully so; I had thoughts of hopelessness and suicide daily. I was filled with a dangerous cocktail of emotions—rage, anger, and fear, just to name a few. I was in a constant state of hypervigilance, and I felt confused and anxious most of the time. I could not trust anyone, because, to me, everyone was a threat. I made the decision that, if I was going to survive this pain, I had to do it alone. The last thing I was going to ask for was anyone's help. I had been completely betrayed when I had asked for help after being raped, and I did not need anyone else to remind me how distorted my thinking had become. I knew I was not the same person anymore, but I still had the mentality of a young Marine. Rather than ask for help, I told myself many times that I was becoming weak and that I needed to "suck it up" and move on with my life.

Most nights, when no one was around, the agony of depression and suicidal thoughts had me by the throat. It would pin me to the wall, paralyze me with fear, and send me into a whirlwind of mind-altering, symptomatic isolation. My basement apartment became a nine hundred square foot box of safety where no one would have to witness the cycle of my self-destructive behaviors. I believed I would be safe if I kept everyone else at a distance. Having a residence all to myself meant that I could unravel, and no one would have to see how much I had truly fallen to pieces. It was best for everyone if I was just left alone to lick my wounds privately. Looking back at it now, I could not have been more wrong about anything in my entire life!

The apartment was behind a long strip mall and directly behind a Kentucky Fried Chicken. The smell of fried food filled the evening air every night around the same time. I did my best to recognize patterns of things around me and to try to remember them. The noise from the parking lot would often spark my internal alarm system, and I would notice myself playing loud music to avoid the startled responses. I was jumpy and could not sit still for very long. My level of concentration had diminished, and I was noticing patterns and habits in myself that could not possibly be healthy. I was easily startled and often frightened by being all alone in the apartment at night.

I wanted to remain isolated from others. I could barely sleep anymore, in fear of what I would wake up to. I would spend hours obsessively cleaning and reorganizing my things, just to pass the time. I had horrible insomnia, but it became so normal that I just adapted to a life without much sleep. When and if I did rest for a few hours, I would sleep with the lights and television on to avoid the darkness and the silence. I did not like silence, and the silence while taking a shower terrified me. I had a very intense fear of being naked and alone. Showering usually required me to peek out through the curtains about every minute or so, because I could not hear over the loud music I was playing to drown out the silence. It does not make sense when one thinks about it, but then again, nothing I did then made much sense. I decided to shower with loud music because that was the lesser of two evils. The two times I felt most vulnerable were when I slept and when I showered, and I was convinced that I was in danger constantly. The panic would set in just before undressing, and the anxiety of taking my clothes off and being naked and exposed would sometimes keep me up all night.

That avoidance behavior would then force me to shower the following day at my parents' house, where I felt safer because someone was home. I relied on my parents for a sense of safety and security on the inside, but on the outside, all they saw was my anger. My extreme irritability and anger should have been a sign to someone that I needed serious mental health treatment, but people have a way of dismissing a person who is acting like a total nutcase. I was frightened of the deep dark places to which my mind often went and even more afraid to tell anyone I needed help. It was easier to be angry at the world than it was to be vulnerable to even one person.

The thought of getting employment to sustain living back on Long Island was a topic of conversation between my parents and me. My father suggested that I work in his office, and I suspect my parents knew I was unemployable in the mental state I was in. He was an orthodontist and had a private practice and a home office. My parents convinced me to enroll at a local private college nearby. To my surprise, the school awarded me a grant for tuition just for having served in the military. I did not discuss much about my service with anyone at the college. I let my parents do most of the talking that day. I kept my answers short when they asked about my time in Okinawa. I only spoke when spoken to, still so conditioned to respond as I did when I was in the Marines. I did not say anything about the details surrounding my discharge from the Marines either. My response was the same when I was asked about the length of my service, and I would reply with, "I only did one enlistment." I was ashamed and embarrassed to talk to anyone about what I had been subjected to. On the car ride home from meeting with the school counselors and enrolling in classes, my father told me stories of his college days and how he had joined the rowing team. He suggested that I do the same and said, "It would be good for you to be around other people." I agreed to join the crew team, which practiced early in the morning. Then I worked all afternoon at his office and attended classes in the evening. I wanted to do something that would make my father proud of me again. I felt that I had let my father down by getting discharged from the Marine Corps, even though, at times, I knew what had happened was not my fault. At other times, I remained immersed in guilt and shame, believing that somehow, I had been to blame for being drugged and raped. We never said much to each other about it, but I could feel the disappointment my father felt, and I was ashamed that I had let him down. I thought that maybe going to college and joining the rowing team was a second chance to do something better, to try to forget the past, to let bygones be bygones, and to move on.

I was living to please my parents again, and I was making decisions in my life because of a need for approval and acceptance. I reminded my father during the car ride home that I would not be eligible to receive my Montgomery GI Bill, which provided money for college, due to my OTH discharge. I told him, "I do not know how, but I'll find a way to pay you back for the books and everything." He said, "Do not worry about it; I'll take care of it." Those words "I'll take care of it" instantly sent me into a rage. "Why would you say that, Dad? Why would you say, 'I'll take care of it'? I do not need you to take care of it; I'm just trying to tell you I'll find a way to pay you back. Just do not say that to me again, okay!" I could hear myself starting to argue with him, but I could not stop. The more he tried to calm me down and the more he told me, "You must relax", the more I wanted to reach over the driver's seat and punch him across the face. I sat in the back seat of the car, and I could feel my blood pumping as I clenched my fists and jaw at the same time. I had been triggered by the memory of the moment I reported the rape to Sgt. Anderson, and she had told me, "I'll take care of it."

My parents dropped me off at my apartment, and I spent the rest of the evening alone. All I could think about was how everything had played out since the last time I heard those dreaded words, "I'll take care of it." I sat alone at my kitchen table, remembering every detail of that dreadful weekend in Okinawa. I pictured myself lying there in bed in my barracks room thinking about the rape, curled up in the fetal position and crying. I did not want to shower again, and I certainly did not want to eat. I had no appetite and no desire to get up, get dressed, or go outside. I wanted to be left alone to try and process what the hell had happened to me. I thought a lot about what would happen next. I thought about what Sgt. Anderson had meant when she had said she would take care of it. I had assumed that she had gone back to the office and that she had reported what I had told her to the chain of command. I had hoped that she would stop by my barracks room to check on me, but she never did.

The feeling of loneliness I was experiencing in my kitchen that night in the apartment was the same feeling I had experienced over those four days alone in my barracks room. I sat at the table in a daze and drifted off to a place that was still all too familiar. Isolating one's self in the memory of one's trauma is the quickest way to madness. I was alone with my thoughts, and it played out in my head like a nature show on the Discovery Channel. My mind raged like a wild set of waves that reached unimaginable heights in the center of the ocean. I felt the weight of mental illness creeping in, but there was not a damned thing I could do about it! Relying on routines like work was something I had adapted to well as a civilian. Otherwise, with too much idle time, my mind would hold me hostage in a war zone of memories. Yet the loneliness persisted, and the intrusive thoughts only increased. My head was a self-destructive place that I had learned to occupy with constant stimuli from the time I woke to the time I rested, and I did everything in my power to stay as busy as possible while bleeding out from the invisible wound.

THE DEATH KNOCK
Shara French

A ringing phone startled me from my sleep. Knocking a book off the nightstand, with a jolt I grabbed the receiver. "Hello?" It was 0700 on Tuesday, September 11th, 2001.

She spoke each word fast but heavy, "Wake up, Shara. Turn on the TV," said a familiar voice. My good friend 1st Sergeant LaChappelle was calling from Virginia. The tone of her voice was low, and her words were measured.

"A plane just crashed into the Twin Towers," she said.

My eyes shot open and I bolted to the living room. No thinking, and with gut reaction, I snatched the remote from my husband's empty easy chair and flipped the TV on straight to the news.

My 17-year-old stepdaughter Heather and 3-month-old grandson, Daniel, were still asleep. I must have woken her as I flew down the hallway to the living room. But I didn't hear her stir. My twin nieces and nephew, Corie, Carlie and Anakin, all still in diapers, were just waking up in their room. They saw me rip down the hallway. "Aunt Shawa, can we get up?" said the toddler in charge, Carlie.

I retired from the Marine Corps, as a Gunnery Sergeant, in January that year. My husband, Master Gunnery Sergeant Doug French and I rented a cute 4-bedroom house in the Peppertree development behind the Oceanside airport. He built a lattice patio covering the back porch. I planted passionflowers and honeysuckle vines attracting hummingbirds, bees and butterflies. Most days, the kids rode around in their plastic cars and played dolls in the backyard while Heather and I played the card game, gin rummy. She kicked my butt almost every time.

In the Marines, my husband's Military Occupational Specialty, (MOS), was infantryman. The infantrymen, or nickname "grunts," were the men on the ground who trained daily to engage the enemy. Doug was the duty expert in all things pertaining to an infantryman. His reputation for this knowledge and advice preceded his presence. I was damn proud of him and honored to be his wife. At the time, Doug had around 20 years in the Marine Corps and was stationed in 29 Palms. He lived in 29 during the week and was home most weekends. It was a peaceful existence until that September day.

From down the hallway, I heard Carlie again, the darkhaired spirited twin say, "Aunt Shawa, I'm uuuup..."

With my eyes riveted to the TV I said, "Okay sweetie. Play in your room for a little while. I'll call you when breakfast is ready, okay?"

"Okaaay...," Carlie said in her sing-song voice along with sleepy giggles from the other little ones.

I couldn't take my eyes off the TV. And then like a dart, I saw the second plane pierce the second Tower. My eyes went straight to the sky and my heart screamed. It was like watching a horrible movie. But I knew it was real. The horror was here. Maybe it was a terrible accident? If not, what monsters would fly planes into skyscrapers full of innocent people? What kind of diabolical minds would even think to do this? Were we going to war? Was Doug leaving tonight? I called him in 29 Palms. He and his fellow Marines were watching the TV too. As we silently sat on the phone in different cities, my eyes and my body went numb as I watched the first tower, fall. It just slowly fell, in sick, surreal, slow motion. Giant dust clouds, curled like waves, enveloping the tower as it crumbled...imploding and crashing straight to the ground with a wicked rapidness. Dusty-black dirt-fog, thick smoke and debris splayed outward, toward the sky as it simultaneously splattered and shot hundreds of feet up and out, splayed horizontally, across the ground. The TV showed people running in bloody business suits holding their cell phones, trying to escape the great plumes of dark gray dust and debris reaching for their backs and heels like massive knobby charcoal claws. I knew they were trying to call their loved ones. I stood there frozen in time in the middle of my living room and just cried. I told the kids to stay in their room.

"Babe...babe?" Doug said, "I'll call you back when I find out more about what's going on."

"Ok," I said. "I love you."

"Love you too."

I knew at once our quiet and peaceful life was going to turn into a world of shit. My life as an American and a United States Marine wife changed that day.

The next few months went by without much coming from the military about what happened in New York. Doug didn't know if, or when his unit would get orders to prepare for a war. If he did, he couldn't tell me anyway, due to operational security reasons. I knew, and I think he did too, that the day would come when he would receive the call to pack his gear. Within six months, he started going on more training exercises to prepare for something. Something? He was training to go to war in Iraq. It was just a matter of time.

Doug would be leaving soon because I understood military culture. The call goes out; you have 24 hours, if that, to pack your trash and go wherever they tell you to. Doug went on training exercises for weeks at a time in the Mohave Desert. These infantry training exercises increased in frequency and lasted for two years while he was stationed in 29 Palms. In Oceanside, I held the fort down caring and loving four babies in diapers and a defiant teenager who, later would become my angel on earth.

We received the word when Doug would deploy to Iraq. Three years after the September 11th World Trade Center attacks, Doug deployed in January 2004 for an "unspecified amount of time." That was crazy. What does that mean; unspecified amount of time? I learned, after he returned from Iraq, that his unit was on the front lines of the battlefield and facilitated the initial entry into Iraq. Coalition forces then followed the push into Baghdad.

In keeping with the Marine Corps Motto, "First to Fight,"

Doug's unit was the first unit to cross the Kuwaiti border into Iraq. With Saddam Hussain known as "the master of deception," unknown dangers awaited my husband's Marines on the approach to Baghdad City. My best friend, and precious husband, was sent off to the war in Iraq, far away from me.

I was scared. He wasn't. He said it was his job. I waited. No letter. No phone calls. I heard nothing for three months.

The days wore on. The nights were torture. The news was on 24 hours, 7 days a week. I searched military news sites constantly online. I wanted to know every piece of military news there was. I was completely obsessed with hearing from Doug. I began to constantly worry. I tried my best to keep my sanity. I prayed.

The next day started out like any other. I made the kids breakfast. Oatmeal with cinnamon, raisins and brown sugar was their favorite. They always wanted, "more, Aunt Shawa, more please!"

There was still no call or letter from Doug. As I was watching the news and folding laundry on a quiet Wednesday evening, a breaking news alert flashed across the TV screen. BREAKING NEWS; 12 MARINES KILLED IN IRAQ NEAR SYRIAN BORDER. Oh my God...no! I thought that's where Doug was.

My mind racked with images of two Marines in dress blues, and a chaplain knocking on my door. In my mind I saw them standing on my front porch; our eyes locked in grief and silence with unspoken knowledge of a loved one's death. It was a nightmarish vision. The dreaded Marine knocking on my front door crept into my head. I closed my eyes and willed the death knock away. Were the Marines reported in the news from Doug's unit? Please God no. My heart froze. Chills coursed through my body. How could I sleep? I can't. I don't. Two agonizing days passed. Then, I received a call from a military support spouse in 29 Palms with information on what happened next to the Syrian border. She confirmed that the Marines killed were from my husband's unit, but that everyone else was fine. Everyone else was fine? Everyone else was not fine. I was not fine. Doug was not fine. But he was alive.

I cried for hours that day. My heart dropped, then lifted, dropped then lifted again between grief and happiness. My mind toggled, struggling between grieving for the Marines who were lost, and happiness for my husband. I grieved for Doug, and his sorrow for the families of the Marines. That deep feeling of heavy grief stayed on my heart. Doug's phone call was late that night and I woke to the sound of his voice.

My beloved's voice brought me peace.

COLD WAR STORIES

TOP SIDE'S SECRET WEAPON
Pete Peterson

On a warm June evening in 1957, along with 83 other young men, I climbed onto a Military Air Transport Service Cargomaster bound for the Marine Corps Recruit Depot, San Diego, CA. I was seventeen and a week out of high school. In the seat next to me was Gerald R. Hermann. Soon to be twenty-two, Herm had hardly left my side since we had met two days earlier at the Greyhound bus station in St. Louis.

"Where ya goin'?" the concrete slab of a man had asked as I dodged other luggage-toting passengers.

"My hotel."

"I got me a free room, too. Somewheres." His Adam's apple bobbed. He shoved a paper at me. "I'm off to be a Marine. Can ya help me? We ain't got big cities like this in South Dakota. Name's Herm." His grip hurt my hand.

Comparing addresses, we found that we were headed for the same place. Herm heehawed, "Ya gonna be a Marine too?"
With my room key safely in hand, to escape his loud geehaw laughs and country-boy questions, I slipped into a phone booth. "Gotta call home," I lied.

The next morning, Herm was outside the hotel restaurant when I came up. "Hoped I'd find ya here."

After a breakfast of bacon, eggs, and coffee (Herm helped himself to the toast I had not eaten), we walked to the induction center, along with probably twenty other young men, all "off to be Marines."

At the Center, Herm was in the desk next to me while a staff sergeant explained how to complete crucial enlistment papers. When I stood to turn in my forms, Herm asked, "Could ya help me? Hard to see in this light. Recruiter said they'll give me glasses in San Diego. I'll tell you what to write, okay?"

The staff sergeant clapped his hands. "Turn yer papers in. Ya ain't writin' a book."

Herm looked so alone, so innocent; I reluctantly helped him fill out his paperwork. The rest of the day, whether eating box lunches on a bench outside the center, sweeping and swabbing the head under the critical eye of a Marine three-striper, or talking with other recruits, Herm left my side only when we lined up in alphabetical order for physicals.

When I stepped across the yellow line and placed my feet in the white-shoe imprints outlined on the green concrete floor, raised my right hand and swore to support and defend the Constitution of the United States, Herm was next to me. On the cattle car ride to the airport, his lanky 6-foot, 3-inch, 180-pound body dwarfed my 5-foot 7-inch, 155-pound frame. In truth, every recruit looked at least fifteen pounds heavier, five inches taller, and ten times tougher than I felt. *What had I gotten myself into?*

* * *

Somewhere over Colorado, a young lady, dressed in crisp Air Force blues distributed stale ham and cheese or soggy peanut butter and jelly sandwiches. Herm had two of each. Later, he crossed and uncrossed his legs, a worried look on his face.

"There's a head in back," I said.

"A what?"

"A restroom."

He bolted past me. "Just in time," he said on his return.

"My first time to fly. Always wondered how ya took a dump on a plane."

* * *

The fog was thick and cold in San Diego. Troop handlers greeted us in traditional Marine fashion. "Yer ass is mine now. Stand still. Eyes straight ahead. Move a muscle, and I'll send ya to the brig."

For a teenager from the Missouri Ozarks this assortment of men had a major effect on me, alerting me to a diverse universe never before encountered. In addition to the South Dakota sod farmer who shadowed my every step, there were slick Detroit number runners, eager to please Kansas wheat growers, two Nebraska Mormons, a twenty-five-year-old auto parts salesman from Galena, Illinois, a church organist from Walker, Tennessee, a Texas oil wildcatter, a New Orleans bookkeeper and a divinity student from Macon, Georgia. In San

Diego, two Navajo Indians joined us, along with a Guamanian Marine reservist, a Canadian Army private from Winnipeg, Manitoba and a 6 '4", 247-pound All-State football player from Sacramento, California.

Tall, short, skinny, or fat, we stumbled into the mess hall wearing Marine Corps-issue sweatshirts and ill-fitting green caps hiding new burr haircuts. The food was cold pancakes, reconstituted eggs, mystery meat sausage, prunes, warm milk, and cups of brown liquid euphemistically called coffee.

Our drill instructors yelled, hollered, and cussed until we were at the Quonset huts that would be our home for the next fourteen weeks. You guessed it. Herm and I were in the same platoon, same squad. We graduated boot camp on a Friday, then climbed onto buses headed to Camp San Onofre on massive Camp Pendleton, where "real" Marines lived. Here, we would undergo infantry training—50-mile hikes in full gear, simulated firefights, advanced first aid clinics, hand grenade nomenclature classes, and booby trap demonstrations.

Three weeks into that routine, our Military Occupation Statuses, (MOS) were posted. I was 0300, Infantry—a grunt to be honed into an HPK (hired professional killer). Herm? What did you expect, motor pool? Nope. Infantry.

We graduated in late September. While other Marines scattered to exotic-sounding duty stations—Hilo, Hawaii; Virginia Beach, Virginia; or Treasure Island, California, Herm, myself, and three other unlucky bastards headed for Marine Barracks, Point Mugu, a top-secret missile base near Oxnard in central California. There, Herm and I were assigned to Second Platoon, topside. When we stowed our gear, he pointed to a rack. "Mind takin' the top bunk? I'm afraid of heights."

* * *

Our racks (beds to civilians) were WW II vintage with sagging springs. Our gear lockers offered the security of a cardboard box, with locks that would not lock, rusting doors, and bent shelves. Other amenities were equally grand—a shower that spit water from two lime-coated shower heads and a concrete floor showing patches of peeling gray paint. The back ladder (stairs to civilians), creaked and groaned when stepped on, handrails long lost. Each morning, we assembled for roll call and P.T. on a parking lot with holes that could swallow a jeep.

Duty at Point Mugu—Headquarters, Pacific Missile Range—followed a port and starboard regimen, that is, one platoon stands duty for twenty-four hours and then is relieved by the other platoon. Our days were structured around six guard shifts, each four hours long. Liberty call for the off-duty platoon began at 1600 and ended at 2400. Friday, the off-duty platoon stood inspection and then had liberty until 2400 Sunday night.

Maybe six months into that numbing routine, after a day of close-order drill, judo practice, and a six-mile run, I hit the shower. Other Marines splashed on Afta Shave and dashed for the liberty bus. My usual routine was to eat chow at the mess hall after the shower, then grab the 1700 bus to town and hole up at the Oxnard library, returning to base at 2300.

California's sunny beaches were wasted on me; sand sticks to me like flour to a chicken wing, and the sun does not tan, it blisters. The local bars vigorously enforced the no-alcohol-for-minors law, so the library was a pleasant refuge.

One night I stayed in the barracks reading "Exodus," a novel by former Marine Leon Uris. Herm had showered and now slumped on his footlocker in his skivvies, a towel draped over his shoulders.

"You like the marines?"

"Better than cooking at a greasy spoon," I answered. It would have been my fate if I had stayed in my hometown. "How about you?"

"You bet. First time ever I don't worry about bein' yanked from bed and gettin' beat on." He stood, and his towel fell. When he bent to pick it up, I noticed that his back was laced with angry red scars and welts. I blurted, "Geez, man. What happened to you?"

"Dad. He drinks, comes home mad, wales the shit outta me." Herm twisted his mouth. "Broke my jaw, chipped my teeth. I joined up to have money so Wanda can move to town and finish high school."

"Who's Wanda?"

"Kid sister. Sixteen. She'll be the first in our family to graduate. If Dad don't get her."

* * *

A few days later, Herm was waiting when I came out of the shower. "Ya got the 1600 watch, right?" He was wearing the glasses his recruiter had promised.

I nodded. "I wanna send an allotment to the bank so Dad won't worry 'bout the farm payment. That way he won't drink and beat up on Wanda. Ya got time. Could ya help me with the papers?"

He was so genuine, so innocent, that I nodded, knowing full well that I was going against the adage to make only acquaintances in the Corps, not friends. Already, other Marines had questions. Did Herm ever sleep or leave the base? Where did he learn to drive any vehicle that had a motor and gears?

I was uncomfortable with knowing the details of Herm's personal life, especially the money part. I had hoped his new glasses would mean my time as his personal secretary was over. Silly me.
At the company office, I pointed out that, with the allotment deducted from his pay, he would have $6.18 left over for the entire month. He shrugged, grinned, and signed.

* * *

One Monday morning, halfway through P.T., a semi-trailer pulled up in front of the barracks. Workmen unloaded cartons of gear lockers, bunk beds, desks, and cans of green paint. The Executive Officer assembled both platoons and announced a contest. The platoon that painted their quarters and moved in the new furniture the fastest would win a four-day liberty pass.

It was a reasonable contest, but my platoon was on duty, so we would be hours behind First Platoon, who had a training day. Also, our regular platoon sergeant was on leave, so I was acting in his place, though I was only a corporal. (In the Corps, you often work above your pay grade.) I was sure that First Platoon would take a break from training and rehab their unit instead. They should have easily won the contest.

But I had forgotten about our secret weapon, Pfc. Herm Hermann.

By this time, Herm had a reputation as a cumshaw artist— a guy who "finds" underutilized tools, typewriters, even furniture, and redirects them for better use—usually for himself or his platoon. He had also demonstrated his physical strength on many occasions. On burn detail, he had ripped up thick volumes of classified and sensitive material, including the base telephone book, bare-handed, with the Officer of the Day looking on in stunned disbelief.

Now I called my fire teams together. "Team One, carry out the old furniture, then scrub the deck. When it dries, apply the paint. Team Two, arrange all the new stuff into groups near the back steps. When the decks dry, Team Three will carry everything up. Remove the cartons only when the furniture is upstairs and placed where it belongs."

Herm smiled like he did when he was about to ask for help. "Got it covered," he said. Herm had watch from 0800 to 1200, but still, before he jumped into the guard truck, he and another marine dragged two industrial fans up to our squad bay. Where they had come from, I did not know or care.

I had duties to oversee—raising the flag in front of company office, reviewing and signing off on the previous shift's logbook, guards to be relieved, new sentries to be posted, mess call for those not on duty, sick call to be announced, mail call to be made, along with the usual duties of getting the Commanding Officer's car washed and the plan of the day read over the loudspeaker.

When I had a free minute, I ran topside. The barracks was empty, the old furniture was outside, and the new gear was waiting to be installed. Herm's industrial fans had dried the freshly painted deck. Herm came off duty and attacked the unopened cartons with long arms and corn-husking tough hands.

Meanwhile, First Platoon was waiting for their deck paint to dry, without fans to speed the process. To keep everyone busy, their NCOs had directed that the furniture be opened on the grass, which meant that entryways were clogged, and progress slowed. In an example of *esprit de corps*, when our deck was dry and our gear was being carried topside, Herm lent his fans to First Platoon, who had canceled liberty call and, at 2000 hours, still had new furniture to move. The four-day liberty pass was ours, thanks in large part to Gerald R. "Herm" Hermann.

* * *

Shortly after "the Big Remod," as our barracks transformation was called, Herm came up to me as I shaved.

"Got a letter. Dad came in drunk and beat on Wanda. Mom took her to Uncle Don's. Dad says he'll teach Wanda a thing or two when he finds her. Any advice?"

"Not really. I guess you could call the bank and see if they'd loan you the money to relocate her."

"Would ya do that?"

"Do what?"

"Call 'em. Say ya believe in me, and they can just add this money to our loan. Like I borrowed it for seed or whatever."

"No way."

"Ah, come on. One last favor."

With his pain-honed voice, hurt-filled blue eyes, and the realization that I was in too deep to turn back, I placed a long-distance phone call, on my nickel, to a bank in South Dakota recommending that they issue a loan to a Marine Pfc. I hardly knew so that his high school-student sister could take refuge from a drunken father who beat her up. The amazing thing is that it worked. Herm got his loan.

* * *

Shortly after Herm's phone call, I went to the company office to write a letter of recommendation for a squad member who had been arrested for shoplifting women's underwear. While waiting, I read personnel notices. One said that the Corps had a critical need for Marines to serve at overseas embassies. After signing my letter, I told the clerk I wanted to apply for embassy duty.

"You're kidding. Who'd want to go to some flea-bit country and guard some run-down embassy?"

"That would be me."

He handed me the memo. "Knock yourself out, but don't take it out of the office."

* * *

I completed the application on the spot. I needed letters of recommendation from two officers and my Commanding Officer's signature. I knocked on the Executive Officer's office door, hoping to get an appointment for the next day.

Captain La Monte asks, "How can I help you, Corporal?" I showed him the memo.

Twenty minutes later, I headed back to the barracks, my request for embassy duty winging its way to D.C. by official U.S. Marine Corps mail.

* * *

Two weeks before Christmas, 1959, my transfer was approved. I had to be in Washington, D.C. for Marine Security Guard School, on 2 January 1960. In the meantime, there were passport photos to be taken, dress blues to be purchased and tailored, and personnel forms—endless personnel forms—to be completed in triplicate. An in-depth physical had to be undergone, dental work endured, an interview with a Navy psychologist arranged, immunization shots for every disease known to man given, and regular duty pulled.

I was packing on the Friday night before I shipped out. The barracks was quiet, because it was liberty weekend. I set my duffle bag on my footlocker and noticed that Herm was on his bunk, his face buried in a pillow and his body jerking.

"You okay?"

He sat up, eyes red and face swollen.

"What's wrong, Marine?"

"Wanda. Dad busted her rib. Blacked her eye. She quit school and ran off to Sioux Falls to be married." His face was white as his skivvy top. "If I'd stayed home, he'd have me to beat on, not her."

"You did what you thought best." *What else could I say*?

"Yer leavin' makes it worse."

"You'll be fine, Marine." Then I asked, "You can read, but can't write?"

"Sign my name is 'bout all. Never figured out 'rithmetic, neither. That's why Wanda needs schooling. So we stop doin' stupid things, not just be punchin' bags for the Old Man." He sobbed again.

I said, "Take a break, Marine. Pull on some clothes. Let's go to the slop chute and make plans. My treat. 10-4?"

We drank malts, ate Planter's peanuts and talked farming. Herm told me he had tried to convince his dad to rotate crops and to charge hunters to hunt pheasants on their land. Herm had played football in grade school, and his dad had been so proud when he bulled through the other team for a touchdown that his dad had clapped him on his back and hugged him. His mom had cried when she dropped him off at the bus station as he left to become a Marine.

* * *

I slept my way across the country on a Greyhound and got off Christmas Eve morning in St. Louis. I called my Sis, hoping she would invite me to spend the day with her family. When she did not, I walked to Union Station and bought a ticket to D.C.

I dropped Herm a line from the embassy in Teheran, with a stamped, addressed envelope in the letter so that he could reply easily. No reply ever came.

I wondered, whatever had happened to Wanda?

* * *

In September 1997, a little over forty years after I first met Herm Hermann at the bus station in St. Louis, I visited Sioux Falls, South Dakota for work. On Friday evening, in an unfamiliar place with unfamiliar people and a long weekend stretching before me, a phone booth beckoned. Out of curiosity, I opened a directory. There it was: Gerald R. Hermann, Route 3, Vermillion, South Dakota.

I inquired at the concierge's desk as to how to get to Vermillion, and she called a hotel employee over.

"I know that farm; pass it twice a day," he said. "You got a rental?"

I nodded. "I'm off at four. Follow me. I'll take you right to the gate."

* * *

A gravel road led to a white house under a stand of trees. Up close, the ribs of a snow fence punched the gray sky. The yard was weedgrown. The back porch and middle part of the house showed the effects of a fire—the siding soot-stained, the windows boarded. A mobile home sat in the shadow of an outbuilding.

A gruff voice answered my knock on the trailer door. "Who's there?"

"Platoon one sixty-three on the road," I yell in my best drill instructor's voice.

The door opens a crack. "Who are ya?"

"A fellow Marine. Peterson. From boot camp—and Point Mugu. Remember me?"

"I 'member."

"How you been?"

"Not too hot."

"Sorry to hear that."

Herm came down the steps one at a time. He wore heavy boots, blue jeans with suspenders, and a checkered shirt with one sleeve rolled up. A wicked v-shaped scar creased his right cheek. His hair was uncombed, thinning, and sprinkled with gray. His hand was like a sack of peanuts when we shook. He slapped his hip. "Broke it last month. Drill hammer damn near did me in."

"Sorry, to hear that. You okay otherwise?"

"Yeah," He squinted his pale blue eyes. "after ya left for— wherever it was—"

"Teheran."

"Yeah. Dad came home drunk. Hit a steer. Rammed a tree. Split his head open, broke his neck. Froze in his own blood. Momma asked the Marines to send me home. They did. Been here ever since. Momma died five year ago March. Found her body near a overturned basket of clothes. Froze stiff."

"You've had tough luck, Marine. How about Wanda?"

"Died. Cat scratch fever. Doctors thought it was the flu. Wrong treatment for cat scratch; left two daughters. Husband, Russ, remarried. Raised the girls. Lives up 'round Brookings."

I let the medical mistake remain a mystery. "You married?"

"Nope. Who'd want a broke-down feller like me? Hell, lost the farm when Momma died." His goofy laugh was just a memory. He glanced toward the trailer. "I'd invite ya in, but ain't got nowhere for ya to sit. Just a bed, stove, TV."

"What more do you need?" I tapped his shoulder. "I always wondered about Wanda. Now I know."

I drove back to Sioux Falls and stocked up on books, Diet Cokes, and Planter's peanuts for a weekend of reading. It would not be such a long weekend after all.

IT WAS A VERY LONG TIME AGO
Ron Pickett

Part One

I heard it again the other day. "Close only counts in horseshoes and hand grenades." When I hear that, I can't help adding, "—and atom bombs." It always seems to lead to an odd expression on the other person's face.

There is just the first faint indication of light on the horizon. Actually, that is the first indication that there is a horizon. The sun will be rising from my six O'clock position in a half hour or so. My red cockpit lighting has been turned down since right after the cat shot nearly three hours ago. I am completely alone, as alone as I have ever been in my life. The cockpit air in the AD (later A1) Skyraider is drawn from the outside and warmed by the large radial engine that is right in front of me. The sounds of the eighteen cylinders, 2700 horsepower, bathed in 32 gallons of oil running smoothly turning the 13-foot prop in a steady arc, even in the dark, the sounds are surprisingly comforting.

I think about the first time I saw a nuclear weapon, like the one that is currently hung from the center station about four feet from my ass. It looked like a slightly oversized and somewhat fat fuel tank with an unpainted metal surface. (You can see a photo of one if you search Google for a Mk-7.) That was in early 1958; I was 21 and had a mixed feeling of humor, "That's a real A-bomb" and horror, "I'm supposed to be ready to drop that on a target in northeast Asia." This one, the one I could almost touch, I had signed for—a signature line at the bottom of a form on a clipboard. It was mine, but I could not do anything with it except drop it. The protocol, during the loading process, was to have the pilot observe the operation and sign off that it had been done correctly and completely. The ordinance crew was made up of about five men who were more accustomed to manually hoisting iron bombs, or rockets, or napalm canisters up onto the bomb racks.

These early, primitive weapons had some tinkering that you could do from the cockpit – the choice of tinkering entirely intentional.

The tail fins, which were moved together to provide a little extra ground clearance on takeoff, were repositioned after launch to an "x" configuration during the flight with an electric motor in the tail. There were other things about the weapon that had to be done before releasing it. In fact, a special control panel, about four by six inches, was installed in an area on the starboard side of the cockpit to carry out these actions. There were five warning and status lights, as I recall, half a dozen switches, and some circuit breakers. There was also the very important circuit breaker puller; a small metal tool that was included in the prelaunch materials.

Our flight plans usually were for near the twelve-hour maximum for this configuration. That was to keep the carrier as far away from the bad guys' country as possible. It would be nice to have the ship still afloat and operational on our return. I planned about eight to ten targets during the four-plus years I was a "special weapons delivery pilot." They seemed to be pretty insignificant, at least to my uneducated eye. Also, I probably would not be the first person to drop on that target.

There was a full canteen in a canvas case snapped to the back of the cockpit. The water was cold when I launched, but by now it was warm and tasted slightly of metal and canvas. It is all I have to drink for the next nine hours. The box lunch, now pushed snugly against the back of the cockpit, would have been the usual—a piece of cold fried chicken, a ham and cheese sandwich, an apple, a cookie and a bag of chips. At times there was a packet of four cigarettes. I think we had to pay for the box lunches if they were provided by the wardroom, but perhaps we got them from the galley.

How would we escape the "effects" of the weapon after we dropped it? That is a good question, and I was never quite satisfied with the stock answer we received.

Our delivery maneuver was what is called a Half Cuban Eight in aerobatics. It was the first half of what would look like an infinity symbol viewed from the side. The pilot pulls up and goes over the top, rolls 180 degrees diving toward the ground, then pulls up again and over the top, rolls 180 degrees and dives back toward the surface. As a delivery process, the bomb would be ejected from the centerline station at about 45 degrees nose-up pitch, and it would proceed toward the target, following an inertial trajectory, while the airplane and pilot were headed in the opposite direction at full power. I always thought that, as soon as the bomb was released, I was working for myself not the government anymore.

Would we escape the effects of the detonation? I do not know; to the best of my knowledge, nobody has ever tried it. The radiation was not much to be worried about. The blast or overpressure would have taken some time to catch up and probably would have provided a wild ride, on a surfboard. But the light from the detonation, with the brightness of 10,000 suns— that's where the real problem was. "Cover one eye." Yeah right, and when you can no longer see the bones in your hand with your eyes shut completely, look outside. The flash blindness would have been devastating. Sure, people on the ground might have been slightly miffed, but their shooting was not much of a hazard, and they would have been more stunned than we would have been.

As I am sure you know, this is a fanciful story. Fortunately, we never had to launch on one of those diabolical missions, but all of the rest of the details are factual.

Part Two

You may wonder, "How could you do that, kill all of those people?" as I was asked recently.

When I wrote Part One, I hadn't thought about that aspect of the process for decades; in the story, I focused on the process— the smells and sounds and fears and ultimate loneliness from the pilot's perspective. Someone suggested, "It's the warrior's mentality." I accepted that explanation for a while. However, I have spent some time getting back into the mindset of the time. I am not an advocate of revisionist history; I believe that one has to see events from the existing mentality and social norms of the time. Applying current values to a past situation is instructive and occasionally helpful, but it tends to discard and devalue the reality that existed at the time the event took place.

Here are a couple of thoughts: First, we did not really think that we would be launched or that the world situation would deteriorate to such a level. That was perhaps wishful or magical thinking, considering how close we came to a confrontation with the Soviet Union during the Cuban Missile Crisis. Psychologically, it was denial, one of the best resources we have available for self-protection in intensely charged and highly personal situations. So, I take denial as one of the reasons that I could survive and even thrive in that ongoing environment.

Secondly, at that time, the U.S. was committed to a "No First Strike" policy. (Of course, we had violated that principle before it was even a principle.) Still, I and, I am sure, most of my colleagues (or is Comrades in Arms a better term?) held the belief that our leaders would not lie to us and the rest of the world and that we would only launch after someone had hit us with a nuclear strike.

I am not nearly so naive now. Spending a lot of time flying and supporting our operations in Vietnam taught me to be highly skeptical of the pronouncements of our leaders. Test, challenge, research, then do your best to change unfair, unjust, and immoral policies—but still, if you are wearing the uniform, you launch when directed. There was a climate of acceptance and of the belief that our leadership was not like the leaders of other countries. I am not so sure anymore.

Then, there is the reality that it is vital to never look weak in the eyes of your comrades. It was a highly masculine environment with a thick frosting of gentility. Dress for dinner in the wardroom, wear a suit on liberty in tropical ports, and comply strictly with protocol and rank. We sat in the wardroom in order of our rank and of seniority within that rank. The accepted values in the wardroom were, "Never talk about religion, politics or sex," and, implicitly, do not ask philosophical questions. Do not even, for a minute, give any hint that you would not perform to your maximum ability in the event of a launch. An expression of the warrior mentality?

Finally, there is the issue of moral responsibility for actions that evolved from the Nuremberg War Trials. However, those results are not particularly helpful prior to and during a battle. Afterward, yes—I believe that there is a lot of room for individual interpretation of personal responsibility. I do not think most people would agree that each soldier has the ultimate responsibility of determining whether every action that he/she takes will be processed and evaluated in the light of the events at the moment. There seems to be a fairly broad area that includes acceptable moral behavior, a gray area of questionable behavior, and a red area in which there is no safety for actions contained therein. Nevertheless, we do not want military personnel deciding on which orders they will follow. Think through the reality, what happens in times of conflict, and how can we trust the decision-making ability of individuals under such conditions?

So, are nuclear weapons so repugnant that anyone who has anything to do with the design, manufacture, loading, maintenance, and certainly delivery is immediately outcast? I think that the vast number of these weapons that our country has produced and deployed and upgraded tells us that, as a rule, it has been deemed that nukes are moral!

You may wonder why I am telling this story. When most people think about nuclear weapons, if they ever do, they think about giant missiles thundering out of a silo or erupting from a submerged submarine, or a B52, B1 or B2 bomber racing along at supersonic speed so near the ground it is kicking up dust or launching a cruise missile. However, for a decade or so, over a half a century ago, a few thousand single-piloted aircraft with a single bomb hung underneath the centerline played a significant and (if you can read this) successful role in avoiding a nuclear holocaust.

THE FIRST WESTIE I EVER MET
For Brendan and Ethan Quinn
Bob Bowman

PREFACE

The following story is based on events that occurred in late 1962 or early 1963. The Cold War was in its most dangerous phase. The Fleet Ballistic Missile Submarine fleet (then consisting of five Polaris submarines, of which USS Robert E. Lee, SSBN-601, was one) had been President Kennedy's "trump card" during the recent Cuban Missile Crisis. Those of us who manned that fleet were busy assimilating the lessons learned during that crisis, focusing primarily on the question of how to provide the National Command Authority (the President and the handful of people who advised him on nuclear weapons use) greater flexibility in applying our awesome destructive potential during any future crises. Our business was deadly serious, and we took it very seriously. We also had our lighter moments, and this story chronicles one of them.

I wrote this as a children's story in 1998, shortly after our nephew, Brett Quinn, and his family (of Lincoln, Rhode Island) visited Marianne and me at our home in Mill Creek, Washington. Brett's children, Brendan and Ethan, were then nine and six years old, respectively. The boys had a great time playing with our two aging West Highland White Terriers, Britches and Kilty. By the time their ten-day vacation ended, they were begging their parents for a "Westie" puppy.

Neither of the boys had experience with puppies, so, in this story, I emphasized a few of the issues they might face if their parents were to relent. To make the story more relevant to Brendan and Ethan, I applied a bit of literary license to the sex and ages of Dr. John Harvey's children. Otherwise, this story is mostly authentic as written.

Bob Bowman

It was a cold and squally day in the Holy Loch, Scotland, but I was warm and dry in my stateroom in the new Polaris submarine, USS Robert E. Lee. I was preparing the navigation charts I would use when leaving port the next day. As I finished each chart, I folded it carefully and added it to the growing stack of charts on the floor next to my small desk. The rest of the submarine's crew were also busy getting the ship ready for our scheduled 82-day patrol beneath the icy waves of the Norwegian Sea.

My roommate, Dr. John Harvey, had left the ship a few hours earlier to shop for personal supplies in the nearby town of Dunoon. Now he returned, still wearing his wet raincoat. Peering from his raincoat pocket was a small furry white face with a black nose, two widely set sparkling black eyes, and two very alert ears. The face looked up at John and said, "Arf." John reached into his pocket, carefully lifted the eight-week-old "Westie" puppy out and put him on the floor.

Having been in John's pocket for more than an hour, the first thing the puppy did was to explore our stateroom. He quickly found the stack of charts and peed on them. Then he turned and looked at me. He cocked his head to one side, then the other. Then he got down on his "elbows," stuck his rump in the air, wagged his tail, and said, "Arf---Arf." The message was unambiguous; he was saying, "Let's play—Now, please."

I couldn't resist. John had bought a small ball with a bell in it, and we tried playing with that. But the puppy had never seen a ball before, so he didn't know what to do with it or how much fun it could be. So, we found a rag and played "tug-of-war." That was great fun! The puppy's little teeth were very sharp. He loved using them to hold onto the rag, and he did not understand that they could hurt a lot if he happened to grab my hand instead of the cloth, so I had to be very careful as we played. Soon the puppy got tired, but before going to sleep, he peed on my charts again. We definitely had to do something about that, because, without navigation charts, I would never be able to find my way out to sea and back again.

The puppy did not have a name yet. John decided he would get the crew to help name him, but that would take a little time.

The next day we left port, shut the hatch, and submerged. We would spend the next 82 days in the submarine together—143 men and one "Westie" puppy.

A couple of days later, we were still getting accustomed to being submerged at sea when we found a small leak in the hydraulic system that raises the periscopes. A crewman immediately repaired it but got his hands very dirty with the oil and grease around the leak. So, he set a can of a hand cleaner called MoBo on the floor, cleaned his hands, and then dried them with a rag. The container of MoBo was a little bigger than a tuna fish can, and the puppy watched the activity with great interest. It was play time again!

The puppy stole the open can of MoBo and took it under the periscope stand, out of our reach, where he ate the remaining contents. He then came out and said, "Bbuuurrrrrppp." We didn't know how harmful that hand cleaner might be for him, and we didn't want to take any chances, so John made the puppy drink some hydrogen peroxide. He immediately threw up the hydrogen peroxide and all the hand cleaner he had eaten.

The puppy was soon feeling better, and now he had a name. We called him MoBo.

John and I soon learned that the control room was a much better place for MoBo to live than our stateroom was. It was much bigger, and there were always people for MoBo to play with and to clean up after him.

Also, the captain's stateroom was only a few feet from the control room, and the captain had a great pair of slippers. MoBo learned that he could sleep on them, or chew on them, or play "tug-of-war" with them, or hide them. What a versatile toy! It was quite common to see him, holding his head as high as he could to keep from tripping over his prize, carrying one of the captain's slippers into the control room to play. If the captain's slippers were gone because he was wearing them, the captain's shoes would be there to chew. The captain's stateroom was a favorite hangout for MoBo.

Of course, the captain soon learned a lesson too. If you are going to bring a "Westie" puppy along to sea for two and a half months, it is a good idea to bring more than one pair of slippers.

There was an awful lot of learning going on!

By the time we surfaced and returned to port, MoBo had learned a lot about submarines and had made some good friends among the crew—but he had also forgotten that there was a whole wonderful world outside the submarine. As soon as possible, John took him ashore so that he could rediscover the pleasures of grass and trees and use his very sensitive nose to investigate all those exciting smells that only a dog can detect. He was delighted to be ashore and to have his submarining days behind him.

Two days later, we turned the submarine over to our relief crew. At the Change of Command ceremony, Captain Joe Williams awarded MoBo his Polaris Patrol Pin and attached it to his collar. Then we boarded an airplane to return to the United States. MoBo again rode in John's pocket and hoped that he would not have to spend as much time learning about airplanes as he had spent learning about submarines. Soon we got to New London, Connecticut, where MoBo met the rest of John's family, including two boys, ages nine and six. MoBo's life was getting better fast. What fun!

A short time later, John, his family, and MoBo moved to Virginia. I never saw them again. I did hear a few years later that MoBo had been hit by a car and had a leg broken while chasing a ball into the street. He was fortunate that he would be OK.

I don't know if MoBo ever thought of me again, but I have thought of him often. He is one of many reasons that I remember my duty in USS Robert E. Lee with great delight and the biggest reason that Marianne and I now have two "Westies" in our family.

Here's a (now badly faded Polaroid) picture of me with MoBo. It was taken in the wardroom of USS Robert E. Lee (SSBN 601) after we completed our patrol, as we were preparing to return to the U.S. I'm the one with the black beard. MoBo and General Lee (in the portrait behind me) had white ones."

THE SHITCAN BATH
W. Paul Jameson

I was stationed in Key West on one of the U.S. Navy's last diesel-electric submarines. The Navy had stopped building them and was building only nuclear submarines, which, I was told, had all kinds of conveniences. Those guys on the "nukes" lived in the lap of luxury, while all us pigboat sailors still had to put up with the old, smelly, humid diesel boats— but that was life. In truth, we were a close-knit bunch and worked well together, regardless of the inconveniences; we just learned to ignore them.

One significant inconvenience was the lack of freshwater. Freshwater on a diesel submarine had always been a scarce and precious commodity, so we were not allowed to take showers when under way. We had a distilling unit and could make freshwater from seawater, but it was costly, eating up battery power rapidly and therefore was rarely used. Consequently, the only acceptable uses for fresh water were drinking, cooking, making coffee, washing hands and face and brushing teeth. As for the rest of the body, it just had to stink until we got to port.

We had been at sea for a few weeks on an exercise in the hot, humid Caribbean and so we all stunk. Of course, stinking is relative. If everyone stinks, then no one stinks, but that doesn't mean you don't still itch and scratch.

And the problem was compounded because we couldn't wash our clothes or even carry enough clean clothes. Lockers were small; I only had room to store two pairs of dungarees, three shirts, a few t-shirts, five pairs of skivvies, five pairs of socks, two complete dress uniforms, and two towels. I'd change clothes every other day, but after a while, I started recycling them, putting on the least smelly item at each change. After several cycles, however, it was hopeless.

The skivvies and socks—especially the socks—got oily. And in time I got crotch rot and a bad case of athlete's foot. The athlete's foot got so bad that I couldn't stop scratching, making my feet bleed between the toes. Its stayed with me for the rest of my life. I guess my constant scratching buried the fungus deep under the skin, and that's the reason I usually only wear flip-flops today.

On that trip, I had had it. I had to wash, but I didn't dare use the shower; I was doomed. Then one day a machinist's mate announced that he was collecting water in a shitcan (a five-gallon steel trash can for all you landlubbers) from the condensation off some machines in the pump room directly under Control Room, and if anyone wanted to wash, it would cost him a dollar.

Drip, drip, drip—day and night, that shitcan began to fill. It was an intriguing concept, but I kept quiet because I wasn't sure the guy was serious. The machinist's mate was experienced, though, so he waited patiently for someone to take him up on his offer while the shitcan slowly filled. When I finally had reached my limit and couldn't stand my own body anymore, I broke my silence and asked, "Is the shitcan full yet?"

"No, not yet. Do you wanna see it?"

"Yeah, sure," I said, with hopeful excitement. So, he took me on a field trip down into the small machinery crammed pump room, around a corner, and back into a tight place where the lonely, unobtrusive shitcan was dutifully collecting condensate. I peered in. It had water! Maybe three gallons! I thought it was impossible, but there it was—deep, cool water. I plunged my arm in about halfway to the elbow and remarked, "Oh that feels good. How long before it's full?"

"A few more days. Do you want a bath?"

"Well, yeah, I want a bath. I can't stand this itching anymore—and the sweat! I want to wash! What do you think?"

"Don't forget; it's a dollar."

"Fine, a dollar; I'll pay it!" I waited. Drip. Drip. Drip.

It became known throughout the boat that Jameson was going to take a bath in a shitcan. I also let it be known throughout the boat that that shitcan was mine, and that if anyone touched it, he would answer to me personally. The day finally came. The can was full. I handed the dollar to the machinist's mate; walked forward to my tiny locker; got a towel, the cleanest clothes I could find, and a bar of soap; and walked back to Control. Everyone watched me as I approached the pump room hatch, and the Chief of the Watch spoke up, saying, "Ready for your bath, Jameson?" "Sure am, Chief," I said.

The other guys on watch in Control smiled but remained quiet, as if they knew something I didn't. Clueless, I opened the small hatch that led down into the pump room, climbed down, and shut the hatch behind me. It wasn't a real hatch, just a grating on hinges. Guys walking above could see me washing in the compartment below if they happened to look down.

I looked into the shitcan, now full of beautiful freshwater and plunged my arm in. The water was up to my elbow. It felt great. Excited, I took off my shoes, my smelly oily socks, and then the rest of my clothes. Standing there naked, I picked up the tin cup the machinist's mate had left for me and poured the water over my head. It was wonderful. I did it again, and it was exhilarating; my body tingled. Before applying the soap, however, I simply rubbed my body all over to make sure I was completely wet. Then I picked up the bar of soap and attacked my toes. I rubbed the soap between them again and again. They burned as the soap was pushed into raw sores, but I didn't care; I had to wash away all the fungus. Then I worked up the legs to my groin. That stung too, as the soap was applied to more raw skin, but I had to get all that fungus out, so I welcomed the pain. My torso and arms were next, then the armpits that stunk, my neck, my head, and my ears; finally, I thoroughly lathered my hair. I was now completely covered in soap from the top of my head to my feet. It was magnificent. I rubbed the soap over my body again and again until I developed a good soapy lather all over. "I'm getting clean; I'm getting clean," I mumbled to myself. But then—the battle stations alarm rang out: CLANG, CLANG, CLANG; *"General Quarters, General Quarters. Man your battle stations."*

I yelled, "Aw shit!", and a chorus of laughter erupted from the Control Room above. In the Navy, there's only one excuse for not showing up to general quarters; you had better be dead. I had to go.

I glanced at my clothes draped over a pipe. I didn't have time. Forget the skivvies; forget the socks; forget the shoes. I pulled my dungarees over my soapy body; grabbed my shirt; yelled, "up ladder!" to clear anyone away from the pump room hatch; scurried up the ladder into the Control Room; and quickly walked barefoot, bare-chested, and covered with soap toward my battle station in the Forward Battery compartment—while the new battle station arrivals to the Control Room also broke out in laughter.

"Hey Jameson, you're all wet!" said the Chief of the Watch with a big grin; and that was when I learned that it was a planned general quarters drill and that the Chief of the Watch had known all along!

VIETNAM STORIES

FULL DRESS WHITES

Charlie Wyatt

"Why me?" I was asking my friend Jerry, another junior officer on my ship, the USS Saint Paul.

He said, "Far as that goes, why me also?"

We had just been notified that we were to attend a formal reception and garden party that afternoon. I had planned to head to my apartment in Mission Beach as soon as liberty sounded at four p.m. From there, showered, shaved, and sharply dressed in coat and tie, I would hit the officers' club in search of friendly female companionship. Instead, I, along with Jerry, would spend several hours standing around with a bunch of senior officers and their wives. That would involve making bland conversation and appearing interested in whatever they cared to ask us or, more likely, dictate to us.

I said, "On top of everything else, we've got to suffer in those stupid dress whites."

Jerry said, "Yeah, and I hear it's mostly outside, with the sun beating down on us for at least two hours."

It was mid-August in San Diego and about as hot as it ever gets there. On the ship, we wore what were called "working" or informal white uniforms. Those were not bad; they had short sleeves and open-throat collars. Full dress whites were another story. The material was much thicker and stiff. The worst part was that the collar buttoned up tight high on the neck, just under the chin.

"Another thing," I said, still resenting the disruption of my plans for the evening "the only women there will be the wives of the senior officers. You can bet they'll be watching like hawks for anything they think is 'not appropriate.' It's like walkin' on eggshells."

At twenty minutes to five, properly attired in our formal best, Jerry and I climbed into his older Ford sedan and headed for Nimitz Boulevard. That was where several senior captains had their residences. When we arrived at the designated address, a uniformed enlisted man directed us where to park. We walked to the front door of a large two-story house set well back from the street.

We entered the front hall, and we each deposited a calling card on the silver tray sitting on a small antique table. Yes, in those stiff, formal days, officers were required to have "calling cards" stating name and rank for just such occasions. In the event that there was more than one lady resident in the household, we were required to leave a card for each.

A maid conducted us down the hall and out a rear entrance to a large expanse of perfectly trimmed green lawn, bordered by rose bushes. It consisted of two levels, the smaller one touching the rear of the house. On it was a long table, covered with white linen, bearing two huge punch bowls and a multitude of large-handled cups. Still another maid handed one of those to me and filled it almost to overflowing with red liquid.

Jerry and I made our way down some steps cut into the bank that separated the two levels. The lower, much larger lawn was already filling up with officers of all ranks and a scattering of well-dressed wives. We did our best to mingle and exchange mostly polite nothing comments with the guests.

After a while, I became separated from Jerry and found myself talking to the captain who was hosting the party. I should mention that, in the Navy, if you were outside, you wore a hat. That was relaxed in some social situations and I had mine now tucked under my right arm, with my mostly full glass in my left hand. I had tried to drink some of the punch, but it was terrible. The captain suddenly switched his gaze from me to the area just behind me. He said, "Good afternoon, sir. I hope you are enjoying the party."

I instinctively stepped to the side and back to allow whomever was behind me access to the captain. Unfortunately, I stepped on someone's foot, lurched, and lost control of both my hat and the glass. It spilled, not on me, but on the tall man who had just walked up. The first thing I noticed when I recovered my balance was that the guy's shoulder boards, indicating his rank, were almost solid gold.

"My god," I thought, "that's an admiral!" The next thing I saw was a red stain all down his white pant leg. "Excuse me," I stammered. "I'm terribly sorry, Admiral. I--, I--"

There was really nothing I could say. His aide, a hard-looking lieutenant commander, grabbed my arm and force-walked me about ten steps away. Still gripping my arm, he said, "You idiot! You spilled crap on Admiral Zumwalt. This whole reception was for him. God knows how he can carry on now; there's no change of pants here." He took a deep breath. Where are you stationed Mr. -?--?"

"Wyatt, sir, on the Saint Paul."
"Well, Mr. Wyatt, I think your best bet would be to get the hell out of here—the sooner the better. I did exactly that, practically sprinting up the steps and through the house. I found Jerry's car and kind of hunkered down behind it. It was more than half an hour before he showed up. "Hey," he said, "I lost track of you. Hear what happened? Somebody spilled a drink on Admiral Zumwalt."

I said, "Yeah, I had a front-row seat." On the way back to the ship, I confessed.

"Jesus! You could be in big trouble. I don't think they could send you to Leavenworth Prison, but they could send you to Vietnam."

I said, "That's where I'm headed anyway. I start swift boat training on September first. I just hope they don't send me to Adak, Alaska, up above the Arctic Circle."

***

A little more than a year later, I had just returned to our base in Cat Lo. It had been a particularly bad time on patrol of the Mekong Delta rivers, 36 hours with little sleep and several ambush attempts. Every bit of clothing I had on was sweat-soaked, and I was sleep-deprived and feeling depressed about the whole war. My crew had departed for their quarters, but I had stripped off my flak jacket and sat down in the open doorway of the boat's cabin. I leaned forward, put my folded arms on my knees, and rested my head on them. I heard Stan, another boat skipper, say, "Hey man, how's it goin'?"

I looked up and saw that he was carrying some papers in one hand. His folks back in Kansas wrote him frequently and sometimes sent clippings from the newspaper about things they thought might interest him.

He said, "Heard the news? The big boss might be comin' to see us."

I said, "Whatta ya mean, the big boss?'

"Why, Admiral Zumwalt; he's now the commander of all the Riverine Forces. It's right here in the paper. There's a picture of him visiting the boat base up in Da Nang. I bet he'll be down here next."

I looked up with more interest. "What's he wearing?"

Stan said, "Green fatigues, just like everybody."

I nodded. "That's good; maybe he won't be real mad if I spill punch on him."

Stan gave me a concerned look. "You must get some rest, Charlie. You're talkin' even more crazy than usual."

CATERPILLAR LAPEL PIN STORY
Gary Barnhill

Since 1919 a parachute manufacturer has provided a gold "caterpillar" lapel pin to those who punch out of a disabled military aircraft. The informal Caterpillar Club's motto is "Life depends on a silken thread." Tell me about it.

Labor Day, September 6, 1965. My call sign was "Dodge Two" and I was refueling at 14,000 feet over northeastern Thailand before heading downtown (Hanoi) in a Thud with eight 750 lb. bombs. While connected to the KC-135 tanker, I heard "Dodge Three" (Capt. John Betz) in one uninterrupted RT (radio transmission): "Dodge Two...You are gushing fuel...Dodge Two you are on fire...Dodge Two BAIL OUT, BAIL OUT!

Unbeknownst to me, both Dodge One and Dodge Three saw panels blow off around my engine, exposing a severe fire.

I closed the throttle to clear off the tanker and, without checking gauges, seeking confirmation or asking questions, ejected instantly. Total time from Betz noting the gushing fuel to the explosion was six seconds. My ejection beat the explosion by ONE SECOND.

I pulled up the seat handles, which blew the canopy off, then squeezed the trigger, which literally shot me out of a cannon. The other functions were automatic: seat belt opened automatically, seat-man separator straps kicked me out of the seat, and then an instant chute opening. It was a violent jolt as I went from 315 IAS (almost 400 mph) to dead stop instantly. I could see two burning halves of my Thud enter the overcast beneath me.

It's about a ten-minute ride down from 14,000 feet. I pulled out the emergency radio and talked to Dodge Lead (ex-Thunderbird Gayle Williams) who had aborted the bombing mission and gone to rescue mode. I was descending in and out of cloud layers, but Dodge flight thought I was on the ground. They damn near ran over me as they homed in on my emergency locator beacon while I was still descending in the chute. Funny now. Not then. Three Thuds swishing past is a real attention-getter.

The descent was over a tall, thick, nasty forest. The prior week I had to turn the emergency radio frequency guard channel off as a medic, hanging from a rescue chopper, vividly described the condition of a pilot's testicles to a doctor back at base. The pilot was alive but impaled on a tree, and they were discussing what part of his private anatomy to cut to get him down.

That was on my mind as I descended.

An instructor way back in Water Survival School explained how to reach up and cut four parachute risers to turn a stable military parachute into a guidable sport chute (kinda sorta). Now think it's your first parachute experience. Would you really cut four risers holding your life-saving canopy? I looked down at those intimidating trees, thought about my testicles (a lot), and decided to cut the four risers. It worked beautifully, as I was able to guide the chute to land in a small clearing.

After landing, I heard machine gun fire. I asked Dodge to confirm friendly territory. Confirmed. It probably was my own 20mm Vulcan cannon cooking off somewhere in the nearby wreckage.

A while later, Dodge flight went Bingo (out of fuel, out of here), but as they departed, Gayle advised me a rescue chopper was inbound and homing in on my emergency radio beacon. I was golden. (All's well that ends well.)

What the hell; just for fun I shot off all my emergency flares and orange smoke bombs and spread out the colorful red and white chute canopy.

The chopper pilot heroically managed to land in the small clearing amongst tall trees. After jumping on board, the heavy, fuel-laden chopper struggled to get airborne. It turns out the chopper had suffered a radio failure inbound and lost my position until he saw my flares and smoke. Call it luck of the Irish.

I got delivered to Naked Fanny (Royal Thai Air Base Nakhom Phamon) where an indignant USAF Brigadier General wearing Jump Wings chewed my ass upon learning I had cut four risers—"...can't have out pilots cutting risers...blah, blah".

There was no transport to Takhli, so I headed off to the O'club bar. When I ran into an old aviation cadet classmate, he kindly flew me back to Takhli in his personal, unmarked CIA T-28 Trojan. No flight plan. No orders. Just get in and go. Actually, he let me fly as I had trained in T-28s at Spence Field, Georgia in 1956.

Now, my pay in 1965, including housing and combat hazard allowance (about 72 cents a combat flight hour), was $995 a month. The unmarked T-28 CIA job paid $5,000 a month. I resigned from the Air Force when I got back to McConnell to take a CIA job, but how that got screwed up is another story. (I ended up a TWA B-727 co-pilot.)

Back at Takhli, they reckoned the cause of the Thud explosion was a freak failure of the fuel valves to shut off after the tanks were full. The internal bomb bay tank burst, sucking the gushing fuel into the engine hot section, then exploding and blowing the panels off. The CO wanted to send me to Clark (Philippines) for a medical checkup as I had back pain. I begged off. Pilots avoid doctors.

My neck was incredibly stiff from the opening jolt of the ejection. That night in my cot, every time I wanted to turn over, I had to pick my head up like a watermelon and turn it over. It didn't hurt that much; I just couldn't move my head. Fifty years later, my neck is still a mess, my back still hurts, my knees gave out, and both rotor cuffs need babying.

Next day I couldn't turn my head at all, but I lied about it so I could fly a combat mission up north to Hanoi. I rode horses as a kid. You wanna get right back on that bronco that just threw you before you think about it too much.

Never heard of "muscle memory" theory back then, but each flight as I was awaiting takeoff, I would go through the physical motions of an emergency ejection because there wouldn't be time to think about it when it happened. Snap heels back, throw head back, shoulders back, reach for ejection handles and practice this thought process: Throttle-Bottle-Visor-Blow and Go. That's close the throttle, actuate the emergency oxygen bottle, pull the helmet visor down, blow the canopy, and squeeze the ejection trigger. I remembered three of the five: throttle, blow, and go.

I owe my life to John Betz. I still think about that day 52 years later.

First, John put his career on the line taking the initiative to command the bailout. He made that decision in a microsecond. His thought process had to be Col. John Boyd's fighter pilot OODA loop: Observe what is happening, Orient to what is happening, Decide what to do, and Act.

John Betz didn't say, "Hey, Goose, check your gauges, I think you got a problem," which would have shifted the responsibility to me. No, John Betz in a microsecond sized up the situation and commanded me to eject.

Had the plane not exploded and flown on and on and on instead, John Betz probably would have been criticized.

And critically important, John Betz used the emotional tone of a voice that clearly implied: Don't even think about asking a question or challenging my command. Get your ass out RIGHT NOW.

At some primitive brain-to-brain-communication level it worked, and I did get my ass out RIGHT NOW, which was one second before 20,000 pounds of fuel and eight 750-pound bombs turned into a huge fireball.

It's a hell of a memory, which still haunts me many nights when the war demons pay an unwanted visit.

Postscript

Years later, as a TWA co-pilot based in Kansas City, I was sitting in a coffee shop on a Philly layover with flight engineer Bill Wirstrom. He asked where I flew in the military. He had flown choppers out of Naked Fanny and rescued five Thud pilots, including one incredibly lucky guy who ejected ONE SECOND before his plane blew up during refueling. He remembered the date: Labor Day 1965. So did I.

The Kansas City Star newspaper came out and took our picture.

THE CROUCHING BEAST WAS HUNGRY
Thomas Calabrese

On Vietnamese maps, the 3000-foot peak was dubbed Dong Ap Bia Mountain. On U.S. maps, it was Hill 937, and to the local Montagnard it was the 'Mountain of the Crouching Beast.'

Between May 10-21, 1969, the 3rd Brigade's, (3rd Battalion 187th Infantry), (1st Battalion 501st Infantry) and (2nd Battalion 501st Infantry) of the 101st Airborne Division collided with the North Vietnamese Army's (NVA) elite 29th Regiment in the A Shau Valley along the Laotian border.

Captain Clay Spencer was a staff sergeant before accepting a battlefield commission during his first tour in the early stages of the Vietnam War. He had fourteen years in the Army and was on his third combat tour in Southeast Asia. Spencer earned the respect and trust of those in his command with his hard-earned knowledge of the enemy and his natural leadership skills. His men knew that if they wanted to stay alive, it was best to listen to this experienced warrior.

The dilemma that often faced this honorable Army officer was that since he was so much more qualified and skilled than everyone else in his unit, he felt conflicted whenever he had to give a dangerous assignment to some inexperienced 'newbie'. Captain Spencer was a professional soldier and kept his personal preferences hidden from those around him. He knew that one of the cardinal rules of leadership in combat was that you could only hope that your men live long enough to learn from their mistakes. Luckily for Captain Spencer that he had a man like Sergeant Lee Warden under his command. They had served two previous tours in 'Nam, were close friends and had a unique rapport that only comes from facing numerous life and death situations together. Sergeant Warden never questioned his friend in front of the other soldiers, but if there was anything that concerned him, he wouldn't hesitate to find a private place and voice his opinions. The two men never let rank or their egos get in the way of the mission or protecting their men.

Sergeant Lee Warden was born in Louisiana, in ta little town called Breaux Bridge the "crawfish capital of the world" in the heart of Cajun country. He was a hard-living man whose favorite drink was his next one and smoked two packs of cigarettes a day. He was only twenty-four years old but looked more like he was in his late thirties. Lee Warden was burning the candle at both ends, and it was a longshot that he would be around to see his 30th birthday. Captain Spencer knew that it was a futile endeavor and more than a little ironic to warn his friends about the dangers of his abusive lifestyle especially when they were in a country where there were at least a dozen ways to die every day.

On May 9, 1969, Colonel Joe Conmy, commander of the 3rd Brigade called his officers to the command center to brief them on the upcoming mission, and when it was over, he dismissed them, except for one, "Captain Spencer, I need you to stay."

"Yes, sir." Captain Spencer replied.

"This is going to be a rough one, so I'm sending my best company in first."

"Then that must mean that you're keeping my men in reserve," Captain Spencer joked, "Don't worry, I'm not offended." "Nice try, maybe next time," Colonel Conmy replied, "Good luck."

On May 10, *Operation Apache Snow* was launched. It was an ambitious 10-battalion airborne/Marine/South Vietnamese search and destroy mission that was supposed to take control of the area and build an all-weather highway that would permit allied operations even during the monsoon season. Captain Spencer and Sergeant Warden and the men from Lima Company boarded Huey helicopters. After they were airborne two battalions from the Army of the Republic of South Vietnam boarded a larger group of choppers and followed them. Before long the skies above the A Shau Valley were filled with aircraft.

When they touched down and exited the choppers, Captain Spencer pulled out his map and showed it to Sergeant Warden, "We'll head east along the Trung Pham River until we can find a trail on the backside and get to the high ground. Alpha and

Delta companies will wait for us to contact them by radio then make their assault up the front side. If things go according to plan, we'll catch Victor Charlie in old-fashion crossfire."

"First question...what happens if we don't find a trail?" Sergeant Warden asked.

"Then we better hope that we've got a lot of sharp machetes in the company," Captain Spencer replied, "because then we're going to have to cut our way to the top."

"Ever notice how good these plans always sound in the beginning? Then about halfway through the mission, things start unraveling like a cheap sweater in the rain." Sergeant Warden took a long drag from his cigarette and called out, "Dutton, you got point!"

The soldiers moved out in single file along the riverbank and since they were heavily weighted down with ammunition and assorted gear, it was a continuous struggle to move through the soft mud that sucked at their boots. The company had gone 1000 meters, and the men were soaked with sweat and breathing heavily. They welcomed the break when Corporal Dutton turned to the man behind him, "Hold up, I might have something. Pass the word."

Captain Spencer and Sergeant Warden moved up from the middle of the column until they reached Corporal Dutton who pointed at a steep, narrow trail, "What do you think?"

The trail wasn't wide enough for an entire rifle company with fully loaded packs to make it through because the triple canopy of jungle vegetation was much too thick. Captain Spencer looked at Sergeant Warden, "What do you think...a couple squads carrying only ammunition and minimal gear might be able to squeeze through."

"Maybe, but what happens when we get to the top, and we're outnumbered?" Sergeant Warden replied,

"You said that plans have a way of falling apart, if it makes you feel any better, at least you can say that you were right."

"I'm just overjoyed, can't you tell?" Sergeant Warden smiled mischievously.

"Ask for volunteers, I need 20 men," Captain Spencer said.

"Does that 20 include you and me?"

"It always does," Captain Spencer said.

Captain Spencer turned to First Lieutenant Rosen, "Take the men back and rendezvous with Alpha Company. I'll radio in two hours; my call sign will be *Comanche Rain*."

"Yes sir," Lt. Rosen moved out.

"The mountain trail was clogged with fallen trees with tangles of bamboo and vines. Sergeant Warden took point and began chopping at the vegetation. After fifty yards of exhaustive effort, he handed the machete to the soldier behind him, took a long gulp from his canteen and wiped his face with the faded green towel that was hanging around his neck.

Captain Spencer approached, "How's it going?"

"Slow and slower, but we'll make it." Sergeant Warden answered.

At the two-hour mark, Captain Spencer radioed back with a progress report, "This is Comanche Rain, we're heading up the hill, but I don't know how long it will be before we're in position."

Lieutenant Colonel Wesley Honeywell responded, "It doesn't matter, Division ordered me to start the assault on Hill 937 at sunrise tomorrow morning regardless of where you are."

"Roger that," Captain Spencer ended the radio trans-mission and pondered the situation.

"What's going on?" Sergeant Warden asked.

"Alpha and Delta companies aren't going to wait."

"Then we're heading back down?" Sergeant Warden saw that his friend had something else on his mind, "But we're not going back down are we?"

"I won't give the order to continue unless you're on board," Captain Spencer offered, "It's your call."

"If we turn around, then they'll probably just send us right back up again, and this way is a lot less crowded."

Captain Spencer, Sergeant Warden, and the other soldiers continued up the hill until it began to get dark then they dug in for the night. At daylight, the men awakened and prepared to continue on their trek. As they started on their way, naval gunfire and Air Force jets began hammering the enemy's positions.

Back on the other side of the mountain, Spc. 4 Paul Nielsen of Bravo Company was on a scouting patrol when he noticed three dead North Vietnamese soldiers who had been killed by artillery. A Kit Carson scout (VC defector) searched the bodies and found documents that clearly upset him. These men were members of the infamous 29th NVA Regiment, 'Pride of Ho Chi Minh' who had a reputation for being 'big American killers.'

It didn't take long to find out how brutal this battle was going to be. As the two Army companies began moving up the mountains, NVA soldiers began popping out of spider holes that were strategically placed all over the face of the mountain. Some were firing AK-47s while others had rocket-propelled grenade launchers. One RPG hit Private Rizzo in the chest, and it detonated the Claymore mine that he was carrying, killing him instantly. The explosion also blew Lieutenant Denton ten feet into the air, seriously wounding him. Medics rushed to his aid as the NVA hosed down the area with machine-gun fire and rocket-propelled grenades exploded among the tree branches showering shrapnel on the Americans below.

Unable to move forward, the soldiers staggered back down the hill while dragging the wounded behind them. The NVA were cunning enough to have some of their men stay hidden in their spider holes and tunnels until the Americans started their retreat then popped up and began shooting them. The soldiers could not go forward or backward without running into gunfire. When Sergeant Herbert saw a NVA soldier pop up right before him, he had no choice but to jump into the hole and kill the enemy fighter with his bare hands. The spider holes were connected by an elaborate tunnel complex, so Sergeant Herbert squeezed his way through the dirt passageway and shot three more NVA soldiers with his .45 pistol before surfacing twenty feet away.

On the other side of the mountain, Captain Spencer and his men were trying desperately to reach the top since they knew by now how bad things had become from their radio communications with the other units. Corporal Nugent was walking point when he heard a noise up ahead, so he gave the hand signal to stand fast and stay silent. Captain Spencer and Sergeant Warden made their way to Nugent's position and he pointed to a machine gun emplacement with ten NVA soldiers located twenty-five yards ahead. Captain Spencer pulled out his K-Bar knife and the other soldiers did the same. Everyone knew that they were getting close to fortified NVA positions so from this point on they would have to be both silent and deadly. The Americans crawled up to within ten feet of the enemy then charged them in a surprise attack, and after a quick fight, the North Vietnamese soldiers were killed.

Every American would have been content to stay safe and hidden in this heavily fortified bunker and let the battle proceed without them, but content and safe wasn't going to cut it on this deadly day on the 'Crouching Beast'. They disabled the machine gun then moved on to eliminate twenty more enemy soldiers and two more machine guns before escaping back into the jungle.

The Americans heard the distinctive sounds of 120mm mortars being fired then spotted the location where several mortars tubes were placed near the crest of the mountain. Sergeant Warden immediately got on the radio and relayed the coordinates for an artillery strike. The mortar tubes were destroyed when several high explosive rounds rained down on them.

"These guys must have a re-supply route, we must find it," Captain Spencer whispered to Sergeant Warden.

"Roger that," Sergeant Warden agreed.

It took less than an hour for the Americans to find it. The North Vietnamese had cut an entire road up the side of the mountain then built a thick canopy with tree branches and vines to obscure it from view. Captain Spencer pulled out his binoculars and saw a long line of men loaded like pack horses coming from the direction of the Laos border. Artillery and aircraft began hammering the area, and with methodical precision, Captain Spencer walked the bombardment all the way down the hill to the banks of the Trung Pham River. With their supply route disabled, the North Vietnamese had no choice, but to continue the battle with their remaining supplies and ammunition. This was good news for the Americans, but there was also bad news; since the North Vietnamese main path of escape had just been destroyed, they would have no other choice but to stand their ground and fight to the death.

Captain Spencer and his men were going on their fourth day in the jungle and getting low on food and water so each time they killed enemy soldiers, they scavenged for anything that they could eat and drink. The NVA had positioned snipers in the trees, but luckily for Captain Spencer, he had excellent marksman among his 20 men, and they began picking off enemy fighters with deadly accuracy.

On the other side of the mountain, 1st Battalion 506th Infantry launched another attack, but a combination of rugged terrain, high elephant grass and stiffening enemy resistance prevented the Americans from getting any further than halfway up the hill. They dug in for the night only to be awakened by a monsoon deluge that turned dirt into mud three feet deep. Mudslides and floods roared down the slopes carrying helpless Americans with them. Soldiers hung on to tree stumps and dug their toes and rifle butts into the goo and hung on for dear life. They were less than five hundred yards from the crest of the hill, but it might as well have been a million miles away. When the rain stopped, and the sun came up, it exposed an eerie landscape; everything was burnt, bent or twisted. Nothing green remained, and soldiers were walking around like robots, void of emotion and drained of strength and staring blankly into the abyss.

Captain Spencer and his men had found refuge inside a mortar bunker that they had captured from an enemy squad. The water was up to their waist, and dead enemy bodies were floating around them.

"The next time I tell you we Must get the hell out of Vietnam, listen to me," Sergeant Warden grumbled and when he reached into his pocket, he found that his cigarettes were waterlogged so he tossed them aside.

"Next time," Captain Spencer, "Where would you want to go instead?"

"I'm undecided between Bolivia and Australia."

"You keep thinking, and when you make up your mind, get back to me." Captain Spencer peered out and saw NVA soldiers rushing about and assumed that they were preparing for another assault. His fellow soldiers were dug in about five hundred yards down the slope and to take every inch of remaining terrain was going to be very costly in American lives.

The American officer had asked a lot from his men, and they had given him everything they had. Fighting with guns, knives and their bare hands, they somehow found a way to keep going, and after seven days on this hellacious hill, they were bloodied, muddied, hungry and completely exhausted. If anyone deserved a rest, it was these noble warriors, but Captain Spencer was going to ask even more of them ...much more. "What do you think...are we up for one more battle?"

One by one, the soldiers nodded their head and checked their weapons. Captain Spencer crawled out of the bunker and was followed by his men. When every soldier was in position, they charged down toward the command bunker, firing as they went. The NVA fighters were caught off-guard, and the Americans killed dozens of them before engaging in close-quarters fighting with the leadership of the elite 29th Regiment inside the underground structure.

The Americans were now surrounded on all sides by North Vietnamese fighters with no escape. Captain Spencer turned to his friend, "Broken Arrow! Broken Arrow!"

"We'll be killed by incoming," Sergeant Warden reminded his commander.

Captain Spencer fired a burst of gunfire into a group of approaching fighters, "We'll probably already be dead by then. Put the fire order in for a **Hamburger Hill with everything on it!**" Sergeant Warden called in airstrikes, artillery and naval gunfire directly on their position then the Americans burrowed deep into the ground with prayers on their lips and the slimmest of hopes in their hearts. When the barrage ended, Captain Spencer and his men crawled out of their impromptu coffin and surveyed the massive destruction and human carnage that surrounded them.

Spitting out a mouthful of debris, Sergeant Warden quipped, "I'm not sure, but I think today might be Mother's Day," then pulled out a bloody North Vietnamese flag and held it up, "I think mom might like this, she can hang it up in the living room next to the Thunder Road movie poster. I'll make up some excuse for the late delivery."

"Most mothers prefer flowers or candy," Corporal Mallory commented.

"You ain't never met my Ma; she takes morning walks in the swamp and hunts gators with a kitchen knife," Sergeant Warden smiled.

"That explains a lot about you," Corporal Mallory laughed. "I sure hope they don't blame us for this mess," Private Browning commented as he pulled out a six-inch splinter from his bloody forearm and sat down on a splintered tree stump.

Captain Spencer waved to his fellow soldiers down the hill to let them know that it was now safe to make their final ascent. He turned to the baby-faced soldier who had aged a lifetime since he set foot in the A Shau Valley. "If anybody ever asks you what happened on this mountain, don't try to explain it; just say that 'The Crouching Beast Was Hungry' and walk away.

WHEN THEY'RE ALL GONE
Leif K. Thorsten

A young boy holds his grandfather's hand while the old man wipes a tear. They have stopped before the monument and he is counting back the years.

He had been in that terrible war when the world had been torn apart. His grandson will never truly know the sorrow in the old man's heart.

For the old man never talked much and his stories were lost to time. So it goes for most generations when long ago events become benign.

How will our history account for itself if no one remains to sing the songs? Who will tell us the stories when the storytellers are gone?

I WISH I HAD
Leif K. Thorsten

I listened to the silence and whispers echoed in my mind. I recalled all
the blessings I owed you and your kind.
I wish I had taken the time to look upon your face.
I regret never caring enough
to understand the sacrifices made.
I wish that I had met you or, at least, had shaken your hand and I will
always be grateful
that you helped to save our land.
I stand before your marker now, your name my fingers trace.
I wish I had known you, before your final resting place.

GRATEFUL FOR THE NAMELESS
Leif K. Thorsten

Those who built this great land, names not found in history at all,
were not the rich ones we remember not those in books who stood
tall.
They were the nameless immigrants upon whose backs,
stained with sweat, did labor the day and all night long, and those
who remain unknown yet.
They carved out a great nation in factories, on farms, and on
waterways.
They bled on the fields of battle so that our Grand Old Flag should
wave.
The women who raced against the sun to keep us housed and clothed
and fed, who wept at the headstones of loved ones while providing us
our daily bread.
T'was the common man and woman for centuries who remain so ever
more the nameless and faceless souls whose toil we are grateful for.

SPECTERS FROM THE AGE OF AQUARIUS
Robert John Buck

I am in shock and awe when I conjure up the realization that 1967 was fifty years ago. I'm sure that many of my fellow 'baby boomers' can share with me the amazement that the era is so far bygone. To me, the era was a cornucopia of mixed emotions and feelings, punctuated by a cultural and political upheaval unprecedented in nature and tumultuous in pulse.

The best way to portray the deserved description has already been claimed by literary artisan and master, Charles Dickens. He skillfully used it to open his masterwork, "A TALE OF TWO CITIES." The opening still makes me shudder, especially when I find comparisons to the aforementioned era. "It was the best of times; it was the worst of times."

The bittersweet nature of that era emits a sweet and sour memory that still haunts me today in its vividness in my memory. The tidal wave of my emotions toward it varies from extreme anger to loving reminiscence. The sweet and sour combination rivals the perfection of ketchup and mustard on a cheeseburger.

Being a Vietnam Veteran, in an era like that, dealt me much rejection because my conservative ways were so contrary to mainstream thinking. I'd often be called to task on my opinions because they did not coincide with those of my critics. The critics included family, many friends, associates, and romantic interests.

I've found, in my seventy years, that women are generally more verbal with their emotions. Men seem to place more stress on actions than words . . . I know I do. This can and has cost me in my life. Many women have thought of me somewhat as an enigma. They have tried to dismantle me, analyze the parts, and come to their own conclusions on what I'm all about. Usually, I think, they come to the wrong end. I have a 'just ask me' policy, and I'll do my best to answer truthfully. You may not agree, but like at Baskin & Robbins, there are many flavors to go around.

In 1966, I returned to the U.S. from Vietnam when the late August weather was readying itself for the chill of the onset of autumn. I had about a month's leave to use up before going back to finish my nine months of active duty in the 'Corps.' I went back to Massachusetts to visit family and friends and to approach a sense of normality in my life. I wasn't quite prepared for the winds of change I experienced! It was like I was returning to a different planet! Even though I was only nineteen, I'm sure many of the differences I saw were a result of my own jaded perceptions, molded by the experiences and recollections of the past year.

I found within myself a new hardness that I wasn't sure I was totally comfortable with. My tolerance threshold had also changed dramatically in many areas. Many times, different people told me I had a very 'short fuse' . . . and I thought that was accurate. but justifiable due to some of my past year's experiences.

Often, I wouldn't speak of these things because most weren't really interesting, and I avoided opening up unless given a 'full-court press'. I erected many inside walls as a matter of simple survival in this new world I found myself in. I felt like an alien in an area in which I was once a native.

I enjoyed the era's music immensely, but often the lyrics and the mind process that created them escaped me. Even so, the music made me feel good... like a severe pain when it stops throbbing. It gave me the feeling that I could alter the mindset that mandated and dictated that pain was a weakness and should only be dealt with one way; bite the bullet!

Often, when I contrast my thought processes of then, and now, I realize there are as many similarities as differences. I think that this is due to a mental growth and maturing of my approach. I have adopted within my psyche a far more effective way of looking at things I thought were set. Some may call it three-dimensional thinking, but I think it goes far past that to the litmus test of multi-dimensional thinking.

I was lured into a discussion with an educator about the political and cultural reasons for the upheaval in Southeast Asia at the time. His views and conclusions were largely molded by the books he read and the obvious political slant of his mentors. I angrily retorted that his views and opinions seemed to be largely the result of living a sheltered life within a vacuum. I thought that the utter absurdity of it only grew when he told me I didn't understand what was happening there. I was 'there and lived it'! My views weren't learned from third-hand sources, but through the eyes of a young man actually 'doing it'!

My resultant inner aging became an understanding he could never comprehend.

To this day, I still cannot easily digest the coarse judgmental slur of being referred to by the liberal element as a 'baby killer'.. .the very thought still pierces my heart. The only thing that somewhat exposes that 'lie' as a 'lie' is the very conduct of these liberals today. Their insistence on making the government use our tax dollars to finance second-trimester abortions says it all about who's really the aforementioned 'baby killers.'

In the time since the Age of Aquarius, I've learned one sure thing, 'hypocrisy' is alive and well in the second millennium!

LEGION OF MERIT
BEACH BOY TO BUF DRIVER
Garry Garretson

Jay Oldham was raised in Oceanside, California, only thirty miles from San Diego. He sought out service opportunities as he grew up, even when immersed with surfing. In grammar school, he served on the School Safety Corps; in high school, he served with the California Cadet Corps. He then attended San Diego State University (SDSU) as part of the Air Force ROTC.

Jay met Pat Nichols on a blind date while at SDSU. He joined the United States Air Force on December 12, 1959, and married Pat on January 16, 1960. Pat's dad Robert L. Nichols was a Navy Commander. He entered the military as an E-2 and rose to become a 0-5.

Jay and Pat had twenty-two duty stations while serving together over twenty-seven years. They were blessed with three children, Lori, Debra, and Robert. Jay retired as an O-6 Colonel. What follows are a handful of snapshots taken from Colonel Oldham's remarkable career.

* * *

"Sky King, Sky King, this is Anderson, Anderson do not answer, do not answer, break, break . . ." came the message over the high-frequency transceiver heard throughout the Pacific Ocean, providing updated target data for the Hanoi area. Radar Navigator Captain Richard Borges received the information and plotted a course. It would be a 13-hour flight in the big bomber, from Andersen Air Force Base (AFB) on Guam, to drop the load around Hanoi, North Vietnam. It required in-flight refueling by KC135's, which Colonel Jay Oldham, the aircraft commander, loved; he often bragged that he had never had a mid-fueling disconnect. The Second Pilot, Lieutenant Colonel Glenn Anderson, radioed, "Fueling is complete, Colonel." After pulling in the boom, the crew headed for the target. The crew included an electronic warfare officer, Lieutenant Angel Medrano, and a Gunner, Specialist Brad Arens. Also aboard were two new trainees, Lieutenants Bart Williams and Anthony Rhoden, observing with a focus on becoming

Radar-Navigators. Bart and Tony would later become C-130 pilots and fly with Jay throughout Southeast Asia.

Upon reaching their bombing target area, the three aircraft team flew 500-foot margins, one-mile separation at 24,000-35,000 feet, to bomb a box on the ground covering a large area. The B-52 could carry 70,000 pounds of weapons. The 500-pound bombs were dropped on surface targets, and the 750-pound bombs targeted underground enemy installations. The crew was always on alert for Surface to Air Missiles (SAMs) and Russian MIG's; there were no SAM attacks or MIGs on this mission, for which the crew was thankful.

After dropping the full load, they headed back to Guam, flying across the Philippines and over the vast sea. The crew tried to get some rest, but the adrenaline from the bombing mission carried over. Upon arrival at Guam, a U.S. Trust Territory and a tiny island of seven miles by thirty-five miles, the crew would see reconnaissance photos to learn if they hit their targets. Colonel Jay was thankful for another safe and successful mission, which they made every three to four days. During one such raid, Colonel Jay's good friend Donald Rissi was shot down in his B-52 by SAMs. He parachuted out, but his chute caught fire on ejection, and he was listed as KIA, Killed in Action. The tragedy served as a constant reminder of the dangers of the missions, and the requirement that the crew be at the top of its game every flight.

After taxiing the B-52 into the parking area at Anderson AFB, Colonel Jay completed his debriefings and walked over to the operations office. He was surprised, disappointed and pleased, all at the same time, to be informed that as of that day's mission's completion, he had flown the maximum number of missions allowed in a B-52, having completed 200 combat missions over North Vietnam, Laos and Cambodia.

Officially, the B-52 is called a Stratofortress, but it is commonly referred to as the BUF (Big Ugly Fella/Fucker). Some B52s crashed while departing Anderson AFB, as take-offs took place over a cliff, from which it was 600 feet straight down to the water, and BUFs take off with their noses down. The Air Force lost two crews off the cliff into the Marianas Trench, the deepest point in the Pacific. All told, the United States lost over 1,700 aircraft to hostile actions, 19 of which were B-52s. All these numbers ran through Jay's mind as he realized he would not fly a B-52 again.

Colonel Oldham would move on to become an aircraft commander in a C-130 squadron. The C-130 Hercules was a four-engine turbo-prop transportation workhorse. One of his first missions in the new squadron was transporting Viet Cong and North Vietnamese prisoners of war (POWs) via C-130 to a POW transfer camp in Laos, an unfriendly country. Although the camp was in enemy territory and there were some U. S. military aircraft in the area, Jay's team was not provided an escort force. When they landed and the POWs left the plane through its rear, each of them dropped the South Vietnamese flag that he had been forced to make while a prisoner. Jay kept one of the small flags and cherishes it to this day.

Jay flew C-130s into every AFB in South Vietnam, and landed at over twenty airfields in country, unloading or loading passengers or cargo (food, ammunition, etc.). One airfield that presented especially difficult challenges was in Danang, South Vietnam. Enemy rockets often targeted American aircraft there.

More than once in Danang, while on the ground and under fire, Jay's crew had to abandon its C-130 and move a full load of passengers to bunkers. On a different but even more dangerous mission, Jay diverted SAM fire from other American aircraft that had inoperative electronic jamming problems, an action for which he was awarded the Distinguished Flying Cross.

In 1973, as the Vietnam War approached its end, Jay's crew transported South Vietnamese generals to North Vietnam for peace negotiations. They flew north from Saigon to Hanoi, up the coast, communicating on UHF along the way. As they flew past the 17th Parallel, which separates North and South Vietnam, Colonel Oldham's co-pilot, the aforementioned Lieutenant Tony Rhoden, looked at Jay and said, "I have a strange fear that the North Vietnamese will shoot us down, kill all of the generals from the South, and just walk into South Vietnam, who'd then be without leadership." Before departing Saigon, Colonel Jay had been advised not to discuss that he had been a B-52 pilot. Upon landing in Hanoi, he understood why. The vertical stabilizers of twelve BUFs that had been shot down were on display along the route from the airport to the negotiation site. Earlier in the war, Colonel Oldham had flown bombing missions over Hanoi in B-52s. Jay and Pat retired to Vista, California. They worked at Wild Animal Park (now known as Safari Park), which is a sister zoo to the San Diego Zoo, for twelve years. Pat passed away in 2018. Jay still attends North

Coast Church in Vista and is a valuable member of our Life Group. I count him as one of my best friends.

Pat and Jay - Hometown Oceanside

Colonel Oldham flew ten different aircraft during his 27-year career. He received the Legion of Merit, six Air Medals, the Distinguished Flying Cross, a Meritorious Service Medal with second oak leaf cluster, the Air Force Commendation Medal, and many other ribbons and medals for leadership and valor. It is my privilege and pleasure to write about this extraordinary individual, who risked it all many times and served his country with honor and distinction.

Thank you, Colonel Jay Oldham!

Big Colonel Jay

Early mornings on the flight line you could see him arrive:
He stood six foot three and a trim one-eighty-five,
With smooth walking confidence and ongoing smile,
Everybody knew you could count on him to go the extra mile.

Everybody seemed to know where Colonel Jay called home.
He lived on the base with kids Laurie, Robert, and Deb. He didn't say
much, he was kind of quiet and shy, And if you spoke at all, you just
said, "Hi" to Colonel Jay.

They knew he came from North of San Diego
Where he was an HS Pirate and College Aztec,
Where he met his true love and wife, by the name of Pat,
His life partner, a fellow student, and a former Navy brat.

Then came the day in '71, returning from a bombing day, The crew
started to panic and could only pray, As the Russian SAM'S were flying
in every which way.
Most thought they had breathed their last, 'cept Jay.

Through the chaos and terror of this real-life hell,
The pilot was a giant of a man that the crew knew well.
He grabbed the controls and began to roll the big plane like never
before. He used every ounce of his try and 10,000 flight hours or more.

Like a giant oak tree, he sat there alone trying to save the crew.
They dropped the remaining bombs which the SAMS locked on
instead.
Next they released the wing fuel tip tanks as a further missile display,
As the crew tracked the missiles on the radar and prayed for them to
stray.

And with all of his strength, he gave the plane another roll.
Then a crew yelled out, "There ain't no SAMs anymore".

And the crew scrambled from a would-be grave,
There was only one who could have saved the day, Big Jay.

With unknown damage from the evasive moves,
They started back down the coast to get on the ground, As the smoke
and gas belched out of gigantic engines.
They landed at Kadena and were met with emergency crews.

They had lost two engines to fire and had shut them down from
disarray.
And everybody knew it would have been the end of the line without
Big Jay.
He greased it into the runway and shut it down, then ordered abandon
ship.
No crew was injured, but they could not fly that Big Buff for a long time
to re-equip.

Colonel Jay never flew that B-52 again and was given his C-130
command.
His Distinguished Flying Cross, ten Air Medals and Legion of Merit
define his brand.
The B-52 crew sent a plaque, with these few words written on that
display,
"We flew with a big, big man, Colonel Jay."

Based on the song "Big John" Jimmy Dean (1961) Columbia # CL 1735 -
(August 10, 1928 – June 13, 2010)

WARM BEER
Charlie Wyatt

In Vietnam, I was assigned to a Swift Boat base near a village named Cat Lo. Five miles up the same muddy river from our base was a small detachment of Australian artillery. What they were doing there, nobody—including them—seemed to know.

The captain in charge was required to send his superior officer in Saigon a weekly action report and a monthly summary. Since absolutely nothing was happening near them, this required a fiction writing ability that everyone in this writing group would admire. I saw one of these reports and marveled at it. I asked the captain what would happen if he just reported nothing going on. He looked at me in horror.

"Gad, mate! They'd most likely send us someplace where the bloody Cong could shoot at us."

As it was, every Saturday afternoon or sometimes just for the hell of it, they would fire off several rounds at the mountainside across the valley. A certain amount of ammunition had to be expended—not the same amount each week, of course—to support the fictitious action reports. After a time, they got bored with just firing at random and tried to make patterns with the white smoke from the explosions. These started as simple geometric designs but evolved. The most ambitious attempt was supposed to be a caricature portrait of Ho Chi Minh, although it came out looking a lot more like the Disney character Goofy.

The reason for my visits was that on the Swift Boat base at Cat Lo, there was no way to buy beer. You could go into Vung Tau, but that was a longer and sometimes dangerous trip. Plus, the only beer you could buy there was Ba-moui-ba or "33." It seemed to vary from not particularly good to downright terrible. The Australians had tons of beer. Something about a daily grog ration, which I didn't fully comprehend, but they seemed to always have a surplus of Swan Lager. What they didn't seem to have enough of was cigarettes. Particularly American cigarettes, which I could buy dirt cheap at the PX. We had worked out an exchange rate: one pack for a beer or two cartons for a case.

So, there I was for the umpteenth time, in our army assigned jeep with my gunner's mate driving, exchanging cigarettes for beer. It was not considered neighborly to just take the beer and go, especially if it was after working hours. You were supposed to share a drink or two with the down under guys before loading up and bringing home the bacon. Or in this case, the booze.

Another thing the Australians didn't have any of was refrigeration. They didn't seem to mind chugging the beer down warm, but I guess somebody told them that Americans had a hard time with that. This one time, the Master Sergeant charged with overseeing the swap had a surprise for us. One of his guys had discovered that if you dipped a bottle into some gasoline—careful not to get any around the top—then set it out, the resulting evaporation would cool the glass and consequently the contents to some degree. Not as good as chilled, but not hot at least. He proceeded to demonstrate, dipping some dozen bottles of Swan Lager and setting them along a bench for the gas to evaporate and cool them.

What nobody told him was that when the gasoline evaporates, it becomes a colorless cloud of fumes spreading out along the ground from the source. That wouldn't have been so bad but for the other Australian walking up just then. One guy proceeded to flick his Bic to light a cigarette. Whoosh!

Instantly the bottles resembled so many Christmas candles flaming away, along with a few of the Aussies. In no time, a bunch of people were rolling on the ground, some of us trying to put out smoldering Australians, while others were laughing their butts off. The Master Sergeant was not amused. In the melee, the bench got knocked over. Some of the bottles broke and the rest were not fit to drink. Worst of all some of the cigarettes got incinerated.

Since it was basically their doing, he felt obligated to replace the ruined beer. Luckily just two Aussies got minor burns, which I would bet were going to be the least of their miseries before the Sergeant got through with them.

In the jeep on the way back to our base, my gunner's mate said, "I got a question for you, skipper."

I said, "You mean why did he dip the beer in gas like that?"

He shook his head. "No, how come they talk all funny like that?

I had to tell him I had no idea.

RETREAD HERO
Robert John Buck

Most of us know what the term "retread" refers to in civilian life. It is a low-grade tire given a second life by a reconditioning process that affixes a new tread to a body that has seen better days. It is not a highly thought-of tire, and its sole virtue is low price.

In the U.S. Marine Corps, it generally does not mean a whole lot more. Usually the retreads are guys integrated into the outfits during a time of an unpopular war. They just show up. They tend to be from an earlier USMC era. They come back because of a number of possible reasons, but—no disrespect intended—they usually have not amounted to much in my experience.

But then there was Paul Vanover, singularly the Marine I have admired most of all. I have a hard time expressing such a glowing feeling toward any male not kin, but here I am, some sixty years later, saying that I loved the guy; I really did! I have never gravitated toward someone so quickly. From day one, he was the Marine I admired most! We were on Marble Mountain the day he showed up at my outfit. He filled me in openly with his brief bio. He had been in the Corps in the early sixties, when little action occurred. He missed that part—badly! When he had got out, he had sought to quench his thirst for action with a two-year stretch in the Merchant Marines. I do not think it quite hit the spot.

The Bay Area resident got the itch again and returned to the Corps. I was amazed at his vast knowledge and was impressed by his views. I was not yet nineteen, and he was probably in his mid-twenties. Paul was a small red-headed guy of vast experience. I learned a lot from him, but I had little to return but a double dose of naivety. Paul loved Governor Ronald Reagan and his brand of politics; I knew little of "Dutch" at the time. Also, Kim Novak was the love of Paul's life; she was constantly on his mind. I could not bring myself to tell Paul that I had only heard of her. Paul was always saying how he wanted to transfer to an outfit that saw more action. He got his wish, and he was shifted to the gnarliest platoon we had. For those guys, a six-hour firefight was R&R (rest and recreation). I ran into him a few times, but I largely lost contact.

My outfit was sent to Danang Air Base for two months of guard duty, which was mundane for sure.

One day a comrade of mine approached with his head hanging.

"Bad news, Bob."

"Oh...?"

"Paul's dead; I'm sorry."

I got a clean towel, pulled it over my head, and cried for hours. Apparently, Paul had been on point in a patrol and had caught the worst of it. I kept the towel with me for the week.

I often think of him, but never with dry eyes. He left a sore spot in my heart and an unhealed wound in my soul. I will never forget him. He was a better man than I could have ever dreamed to be—a brave S.O.B. that I will never forget, nor would I want to. I will remember you always, bud.

WHO ORDERED THIS MISSION?
Dante Puccetti

The 4th Infantry Division Artillery's Headquarters and Headquarters Battery, a.k.a. Divarty, worked hand-in-hand with the artillery in the division. Divarty Survey conducted all surveys needed throughout the division's Area of Operations (AO). Divarty surveys needed to be very precise, because they affected the whole division—in particular, all the guns, both stationary and mobile, and all the mortars. We used T-2 Theodolites, whereas the battalion surveyors used T-16s, which were effective but less precise.

My first survey was at Dac To towards the end of June 1968. I completed the survey begun by my two predecessors, one of whom was killed in action, while the other was wounded and almost bled to death. I performed so well I was awarded the "computer of data" position, second in charge after the party chief. I was a private first class (E-3) doing the job of a sergeant (E-5), until I was promoted to Specialist-4.

One of my most memorable assignments came when my fellow surveyor Chris Blaylock and I received orders to survey the Plei Morang Ville. The powers that be had decided that The Mission before the 1969 Tet Holiday was to survey all the villages located near American military forces based on Camp Enari and around Pleiku City, in order to promote the success of future fire missions. The Mission was prompted by what had happened during the massive 1968 Tet Offensive that had been mounted by Vietcong (VC) and North Vietnamese forces.

Because of the magnitude and priority of The Mission—it came right from the top—Divarty was chosen to complete it. In Vietnam, 4th Divarty was responsible for the entirety of II Core's AO, which encompassed all of the Central Highlands of South Vietnam and was the largest of the four Core Areas. Divarty Survey's primary function was to locate every artillery gun in the division's AO, using the army's most accurate surveying methodology. Theoretically, every weapon in the division could fire effectively at any single target within its range. Divarty surveys coordinated the guns.

Surveying required surveyors to be in 100% combat mode. Typically, a survey party consisted of eight soldiers—one party chief, one "soldier calculator," two instrument operators, two recorders, and two soldiers for measurements—plus sometimes a security contingent; most of the time the eight-man survey party, armed with M-16s and hand grenades, doubled as its own security contingent. Unfortunately, headquarters waited until three weeks before the Tet Holiday to organize The Mission. Its scope and urgency required that instead of the usual eight men, two surveyors—in this case, Blaylock and I—drive into a ville with no security contingent, leaving it to us to see to our own safety. Moreover, the ville in question, Plei Morang Ville, was known to be crawling with VC sympathizers.

Performing a survey in Indian Country with just two surveyors was crazy. Camp Enari had 5000 soldiers, defensive fortifications, artillery, tanks, machine guns, Clamor mines, C-4 explosives, M-16s, grenades, pistols, sticks, and rocks! Blaylock and I had two M-16s, twelve 'frag' grenades, and a radio, and we're supposed to do a fucking survey in a VC ville? Who ordered this mission?

The morning Blaylock and I were apprised of our mission, the sun was brilliant. It would have been a beautiful day if we were somewhere—anywhere—else. It was hot that morning. The heat meant the mosquitoes would be hostile. I tried to remember where the damn repellent was hidden. Its arsenic smell had burned a hole in my memory, and its taste was worse than the smell. Another one of the little things that made Nam a hellhole.

After learning of our mission, Blaylock and I headed out, at 0700, with me at the helm of our truck. The drive from Divarty to Plei Morang Ville would take about fifty minutes. The Vietnamese Central Highlands is a combination of mountains, open valleys, and triple-canopy jungle. In transit, we passed through a tunnel cut through some of that jungle. Vegetation brushed against our vehicle's sides and roof, and hid whatever prowled in the shadows. This was the most frightening stretch of our journey, but why waste my energy looking for the enemy? A sapper could toss a satchel charge* into our vehicle at any moment. Or so I told myself at the time. I suspect I cringed every second.

When we emerged from the tunnel, I relaxed a bit, but the respite was short-lived. As we approached Plei Morang Ville, scared shitless, I stepped on it, racing the truck into the ville. Having created a dust storm, I slammed on the brakes, and slid to a halt in the village center. Using the dust as cover, I bounded out of the truck, fully armed with M-16s and frag grenades. Blaylock grabbed the tripod and Theodolite, which we had pre-assembled, thus saving us ten excruciating minutes. Nevertheless, the clock ticked as we proceeded with the operation, and each second felt like an eternity.

While Blaylock surveyed, I provided security. I looked everywhere at once, scanning the ville. I saw a bush move, and as I swung my rifle, a pig squealed into the open field. Shit. As I covered Baylock, my sixth sense was on 100% alert; I could feel each drop of sweat running down my body. The searing heat, the stench, and the sultry air became an enemy without armament. I wished my fear would negate the effects of the Fahrenheit, but the sweat that covered my body seemed to coat my spirit, as well. Terror split my mind into 10,000 pieces, each dedicated to

*Wikipedia: "A satchel charge is a demolition device . . . whose primary components are a charge of dynamite . . . [plus] a carrying device functionally similar to a satchel or messenger bag, and a triggering mechanism . . ." accomplishing the myriad activities of this singular instant: wipe sweat from eyes, breathe, pray, refocus, swear vengeance on my recruiter, etc.

"It's so fucking hot in this fucking place!" I bellowed.

Baylock erected the instrument assembly—to hell with the time-consuming leveling procedure—plumbed the T-2, shot the angles, and recorded his readings. We then switched roles. Blaylock covered me while I unscrewed the T-2 from the tripod. With each partial turn of the screw, I expected the pain of a bullet. "Turn, you fucking motherfucker!" I cursed the damned designer who made this stinking screw so longass long. My hands were slick thanks to the sweat and filth of Nam, so I could barely turn the slippery screw-head. With one part of my mind, I focused on the instrument, but owing to my combat experience, I maintained awareness of activity on my periphery, too. Finally the screw loosened, and I replaced the T-2 with the Distance Measuring Equipment, recorded the distance to our forward position, and logged the measurement to Camp Enari twelve klicks (kilometers) away. Once we finished with our mission, we jumped in the truck and hightailed it for safer environs.

Mobile Army Surgical Hospital (MASH) units talked about meatball surgery, but this was a meatball survey. Like surgery, Divarty surveying was an exacting undertaking. A standard survey time from arrival at a location to departure was thirty-five to sixty minutes. This one? Ten minutes flat! And our accuracy was off the charts! Our stupidity in taking on the mission aside, Chris and I deserved Bronze Stars for completing said mission successfully.

INSPIRATIONAL STORIES

A NEW WAY OF LIFE
Robert Caudill

(Top-down as service member speaking to their spouse.)
As a warrior standing poised and ready to fight for life once again

From the screams during the night, I must learn a new way of life—supporting you

That the world of chaos behind this is not an easy task when you're stuck in the past

I see the life in everything around us

Is why it is so hard to be with you; over time I begin to appreciate it because

The effects of war slowly fade as the mind and heart heals

This is the hardest battle I must fight

A fearless and battle-hardened life forged in the heart of combat

Bearing witness to the atrocities of war through

The sights, sounds, smells, and fear ongoing in the mind each night

As you protect me from

The nightmares caused by men fighting for a piece of land

Remember to be patient with me as I try to understand

Your burden as you comfort men

This is the life you have chosen

And it is your strength that allows me to grow

Guiding from the dark tunnel with your glow

Comforting me as a welcoming host

As the years pass we create a new path

From these gifts you gave me creating this new way of life

I am thankful as a spouse

(Bottom-up as the spouse speaking to the service member.)

BOOT CAMP: A COMING OF AGE
Joe Ashby

So there I was, wet behind the ears and enlisting in the Navy directly from high school. I always knew I would, as watching *Victory at Sea* about World War II (WW II) ran deep in my veins. A week after graduation, I reported for swearing in, physicals and form filling, after which I, along with a dozen or so others, was on a Silver Zephyr train bound for San Diego. After an overnight journey, we arrived at San Diego and were promptly escorted by bus to the Naval Station. My life from then on changed faster than I could have imagined. I was separated from my personal belongings, and the Navy took control of my life. Other than the civvies I was wearing, all else was left behind in wooden shelves under the wooden canopy at the check-in station, some never to be seen again.

Getting these raw recruits into Navy garb was the first order of business, requiring us to march to various supply warehouses; we learned on the way how to move in a formation. Convention dictated that the tallest people should be in the front of the ranks, which put me near the end. Other leadership skills gradually surfaced, but for those first few days, height was the determining factor. Those entrusted to put us in blues, whites and dungarees cared little about our personal likes or dislikes and used their callous eyes to size up and distribute uniforms.

For me, it was like Christmas. Everything was new and different. Only later did I regret their decisions about what would fit me, as I started to put on weight and add vertical inches in the next few weeks. How small was I? According to my ID card, I weighed 127 pounds, and I was 65 inches tall. You think I didn't pay attention to the bully kicking sand in the scrawny guy's eyes in the Charles Atlas ads I saw in funny books? After thirteen weeks of boot camp with three square meals a day, I'd grown five inches and added over thirty pounds. We received not only the clothing but also a sea bag to stow it in: leggings, boondockers (boots), neckerchief, flat hat, sewing kit and all.

To complete the seaman recruit experience, we were issued dog tags that had our new identity in a service number, and had our heads shaved, even suffering the indignity of having to pay for it. I didn't mind much, as I never did like my hair anyway. Then came the battery of shots. There were shots for everything, and our shot-givers were not too concerned about the pain they caused in delivering the doses in the butt or in the arm. The combination of the shots and the cold night air of San Diego resulted in my experiencing considerable pain and an upset stomach, to boot.

Now they had us where they wanted us. We were totally defeated and having second thoughts about this new life we had chosen. What better time to administer the unending battery of tests to see how sharp we were! The intelligence testing was conducted in the still dark morning when I was starving for sleep and a little peace. How much different might the results have been if I'd had the benefit of a good night's sleep and better health?

Boot camp was humiliating and demeaning. If it wasn't Boatswains Mate 1st Class Elmdorf, the company commander, finding fault with my performance or yelling in my ears, it was the new-found power of our squad leaders. They picked up where he left off. There were rules for everything, and sooner rather than later you were going to run afoul of one or more of them: how we folded or rolled our sea bag contents; how we cared for the WW I Lee Enfield Rifle we were assigned and commanded to ever more call our "piece" rather than a gun or rifle; how we used our clothes stops (strings) to secure our eternally wet clothes on the lines behind our barracks; how we folded our sheets over a thin mattress, with the objective of "military tucks" so taut an inspector could bounce a quarter on them; how we polished our shoes or boots, with the goal being a proper spit shine. The last of these was an art I worked on constantly, trying to achieve just the right combination of Esquire shoe polish, spit and rubbing to see see my smiling face in those gleaming toes.

The 2-story wooden barracks we lived in were spartan. Ten double bunks lined each side of the barracks, with wooden benches separating them; the latter served as places to spit shine shoes, write home, and learn how to break down and re-assemble our "piece." We each had a small metal locker to "stow our gear." And then there was a latrine, known to sailors as a "head." Even there on the pot, in the shower, or shaving at the sink, you were constantly watched for any misdeeds. Of course, walking or marching had to be relearned. Gone were the days when we put one foot in front of the other as seemed natural. Now we had the regulation 45-degree angle that made us look like web-footed fools. It probably had something to do with maintaining the ability to work in gale force winds aboard a bobbing destroyer in the North Sea.

Each day, my life was filled with activities that left no time for rubber necking or leisure. When we weren't in dimly lit, hot classrooms being taught seamanship, naval history, or ship and plane recognition, we were suffering hot flames while fighting oil fires in a large open tank next to the mock ship *USS Neversail*, doing pushups on "grinders" (paved parade fields) so hot that the loose gravel and molten tar burned into our hands, or learning how to survive in open water. Swimming was an absolute necessity in the Navy, and we were tested at length to see if we could handle the challenge. I loved to swim and had little problem, but not so with the non-qualified swimmers. If they didn't swim during the day, they had to do it as an additional duty at night. I was excited when I was tested for my ability to get out of a parachute in the water. They strapped me in a Dilbert Dunker, a bit of aircraft fuselage mounted on skids aimed into a swimming pool. Once I was in the pool, my task was to release myself from the shoulder harness and then figure out how to get to the surface without suffocating under the parachute and shroud lines.

We did get to leave the Navy base once, to learn small arms. We were bused to Camp Pendleton, where Marines taught us how to handle an M-1 carbine rifle—whoops, I mean piece. It seemed to give that young Marine corporal delight when he tightened the leather lanyard of the piece so tight he cut off circulation in my right arm, or when he kicked me as I lay prone, because my supporting arm was not at a perfect 45-degree angle.

You would think that San Diego, blessed with one of the world's great climates, would be an ideal place to go through boot camp. I can't remember a single time in the thirteen weeks that made me feel that way. That is, while we were on duty, and we were always on duty, at least for the first five and a half weeks. This was the period of quarantine, when we couldn't go anywhere alone or enjoy any liberties. We couldn't talk to anyone, go to the gedunk (coffee shop) for a coke or "pogey bait" (candy bars). Meanwhile, the little bit of news we received from the outside instilled fears that the Russian nuclear missiles or the Chinese hordes would draw us into another shooting war.

We all suffered a bit, but some more than others. For example, there was the "company scrounge"—that is, he who was responsible for our unit not passing an inspection. The company scrounge became the target of a "kai-ai party," kai-ai being a stiff bristle brush we used to wash our laundry. During the kai-ai party, we were encouraged to make the company scrounger's naked skin raw in the shower with brushes and scouring powder. There was also the guy who failed locker inspection. When we returned from the drill field, all his sea bag's contents had been thrown out the window, and we were given orders to march back and forth over them. The poor soul then had to wash every item to get ready for the next inspection.

During my company's chow hall week, when we it was our turn to man the base dining facility, I had the good fortune to get duty in the "garbage locker." While some clicked clickers to count how many were fed, and others dished up meals onto stainless steel serving trays, those of us with garbage locker duty had to arrive pre-dawn to clean the large black cooking trays caked with baked-on ingredients. After the meal, we stayed later than everyone else, and deployed searing steam to remove every bit of food waste from food trays and dinnerware. Finally, of course, we had to take out the garbage. All this, and we still had to complete our usual chores, including doing laundry by moonlight, no matter how late it was that those of us on garbage locker duty were released back to the barracks.

Speaking of the mess hall, my stomach was constantly tested as to whether it could handle chipped beef on toast, more commonly called shit on a shingle (SOS), or the wretched corned beef hash and hardboiled eggs, or the dreaded liver and onions. Whether for economic or dietary reasons, an evening meal was sometimes fried bologna. When someone who had already eaten was asked what was for dinner, a favorite reply ran, "Cake and cock, and they just ran out of cake."

Despite all of this, I experienced graduation, during which our company marched proudly, in step, with our banners flying, down a parade field in front of an audience of family and friends. Somehow, boot camp made a man of me. During those thirteen weeks, I came of age.

TWO VIEWS OF MY FUTURE
Art Townley

I stood on the quarterdeck dressed in my service dress whites. Saluting the OOD, I turned smartly to face the fantail, the Ensign, the U. S. flag, saluted again and walked briskly down the gangway. When I touched the dock, I was no longer a member of the U.S. Navy, and at 21, this marked the end of the most life-changing experience of my life.

Four years earlier, when I arrived in San Diego from my home in Bromide, Oklahoma, to start Recruit Training, Boot Camp, I had never seen the ocean—a fine sailor I was set to be. Mostly I knew I had to get out of Oklahoma and the small, unproductive hard-rock farm from which we could barely extract a subsistence for my mother, grandmother, and grandfather. There was virtually no cash. In fact, when I wanted to go to the movies one Saturday afternoon, I took a small metal bucket into the area behind the homestead and harvested the sparse black berries. I took them to a neighbor's house on my bike and offered them to him for a dime. The bike ride on the dirt road had caused the berries to settle and he said, "Look, the bucket isn't even full." I went to several other houses and finally returned to the original house. The wife of the first man bought the berries from me and I was off to the movies.

There is something about a limited life experience that restricts your options; if it can't be imagined, it can't be achieved. The confines of that small rough farm did little to provide me with a world of possibilities. I couldn't imagine what was outside my experience.

My four years in the Navy gave me a vastly broader horizon, metaphorically as well as in reality. I became a Yeoman, the Navy term for a clerk and administrative staff member. I had never heard the term until I was selected for Yeoman's school in San Diego. I have no idea why I was selected for this career field. Ultimately the needs of the service were the real culprit. I worked hard, studied hard, and did well in the school. My first duty station gave me an opportunity to develop my skills and settle into the routine of Navy life.

Later, I had the chance to attend Navy justice school where sailors are indoctrinated into the peculiarities and inner workings of the Navy legal system. It led to my being stationed at Long Beach, California.

Being intimately involved in the legal system gave me two distinctly different views of what was possible to achieve in life. On the one hand, much of my time was spent in taking statements from sailors who were being investigated for violation of the Uniform Code of Military Justice (UCMJ.) On the other, my time was spent working with Navy lawyers. They had college degrees, law school degrees, and bars on their shoulders. They were respected and had a great deal of freedom of action, and they made significant decisions.

The comparison was so clear that even a country boy from Oklahoma couldn't miss it.

I had several promotions with additional responsibility. It felt good and was reassuring.

I finished my time in the Navy serving on an oil tanker in the South Pacific. By the time I left active duty, I had a plan and a clear vision of what my life could be. I wasn't going to work in a feed store or as a sharecropper, I was going to college and find what subjects excited me. After my service in the Navy, I enrolled in college and received my degree in three years with a major in U.S. History and a high school teaching credential.

Yes, I had a girlfriend, and we agreed that we would wait to get married until I finished my navy service. This journey was difficult for two young kids, but we made it. Service in the Navy set a good standard for postponing immediate gratification until the time was right during numerous times in our long life together.

Now, living in a retirement community in Southern California, as I look back on my life, I smile at what I accomplished: Emeritus Professor of history, author of three, widely-used graduate school text books, school administrator, father of two girls, and grandfather of five. I lost my wife in 2017 after 62 years of marriage, which was a terrible loss. Still, as I look back over my long life, it was that four years in the Navy that opened up opportunities and possibilities that I had no idea might be available for me, a poor kid from Oklahoma.

COMMANDER-IN-CHIEF
Larry Klumas

One of the first things a recruit had to do
Was to learn the Chain of Command. That is
Who was in charge from the unit Commander Right up to the President
– the Commander in Chief.

Pounded into the heads of kids who understood
So little, was the concept that there is always a person Over you, in
charge, including finally the President, and If any died, there was an
immediate replacement.

Pounded also into the kid's head, most of whom
Could not even vote yet, was it did not matter Who the President
was, he was always the ultimate Authority, to whom you gave
allegiance.

Quite a simple concept. Except, learning the names
Of each, which kept changing, so when challenged,
The recruit must pop to attention and recite the names
With confidence and vigor, proud to be an American.

So it must be with President Trump, In spite of any personal opinion,
He owns the military soul.

LEADERSHIP
Larry Klumas

Leadership is,
    at its core
        the desire to serve;
A delicate balance
    between
        humble and ego.
Created by
    correlation of genes
        electrically fused;
Tilt toward kindness
    forcefulness
        wanes;
Push desire
    to perform
        follow-ship slides.
How then
    does perfect direction
        score soonest?
Steady eye-contact
    correctly formed words
        spoken sincerely
From Being there
    first yourself - -
        feeling
        knowing
        sensing
    exquisite timing
    rising to
that moments' challenge.

MEMORIAL DAY 2015

Larry Klumas

A country celebrates their sacrifice.
Graves mark their resting place.
Having served attest to their duty.
I celebrate this day
Knowing my freedom
      todays' breath
      being alive
In America
Was a choice
      they made
For God and Country
I honor their sacrifice.
I bless their eternal spirit.

WHAT I DID NOT KNOW
Shirly Turner

We often wish that we "knew then what we know now." Certainly, I do, thinking back to when my husband was on sea duty during the Vietnam War. He was sent over on a carrier twice and returned quiet and tired, but ecstatically happy to be home. We were equally delighted to welcome him back. Favorite foods. Sleeping late. Love from everyone.

During his deployments, I felt it was so important to keep the children aware that though their father was overseas, he loved them nonetheless, and missed them terribly. Every day we sent him letters, notes, pictures, and cards each child made. Sometimes the older children (eight and ten years old) sent diary pages. He wrote back often, with a short message for each child, and an update on as much as could be shared. We waited eagerly for the mailman to bring a stack of letters from Daddy.

Our lesson regarding what we did not know came during the second cruise. The ship sailed in September. The older two girls started school and wrote short letters daily. With no such thing as cell phones or computers, the only means of communication with the men aboard ship were the letters that arrived by plane once weekly. For that reason, we filled envelopes with all the news from home and family, as well as any Sunday cartoons we felt he would enjoy, hoping to keep his spirits up. He often told us that the arrival of the mail plane was the highlight of the crew's week. There were, of course, some problems mentioned in my letters: car repairs, a note home from school requiring the discipline of one of the children, or perhaps an electric bill higher than anticipated. I asked for advice at times and felt guilty for doing so until he told me it made him feel more tightly connected. All of our efforts to keep him happy and connected came to a peak on the evening before Halloween of his second cruise. The children decided among themselves that they would send "lots and lots of candy so Daddy could share." I agreed and bought two large manila envelopes in which to package the candy they collected.

Halloween night, four extremely excited children, sacks in hand, set off: an elf, a ghost, a fairy, and a three-foot-tall football player, all bent on collecting candy to send to Daddy. We were quite successful, and the excitement continued to mount at home. As they got into their pajamas, the children discussed among themselves exactly how many pieces of bubble gum a grown-up sailor could chew at once. As the wife of an enlisted man, I wondered how to mail that candy, and if it would arrive crushed or intact.

Meanwhile, just off the coast of Vietnam, the battles continued. Mail arrived and was welcomed, unless it was divorce papers, delivered in manila envelopes. I had no idea that bad news was associated with manila envelopes. Therefore, a couple days after Halloween, we packed the two envelopes I had purchased. After considerable discussion among the children, it was determined that the second envelope was for the "crew" that had collected the candy. The first was mailed off, and we waited anxiously for a letter to tell us the surprise had arrived.

According to my husband, the week that mail plane arrived had been a very stressful one. Letters, which signified muchneeded support from home, were usually received with joy. This particular day, the names were called and finally came the bulging manila envelope for "Second Class Seaman Turner."

"There's yours, buddy!" someone shouted, insinuating that the envelope contained his divorce papers. My husband grabbed the envelope and ripped it in two, releasing a rain of bubble gum, Tootsie Rolls, lollipops, Butterscotch Bites, and M & M's. After a moment of shocked silence, all the treats were picked up off the deck and shared. The release of tension brought laughter, and for a while Second Class Seaman Turner was teased with "Got any more goodies?"

If I knew then what I know now, I would have packaged Halloween in a box.

GET OFF YOUR ASS
Joe Ashby

"Get off your ass, you lazy son of a bitch", she yelled. I knew she meant it as she had the hundreds of times before, but this time I knew she was yelling it to encourage me to take another step in my recovery. Sally was different; she was special, unlike Nancy, my first wife who tossed my ass out many years ago.

While we were a "beautiful couple" by all who knew us at Long Beach State, Nancy had to suffer through my reluctant facing of reality with the draft, my years of living a false reality among the others with shattered dreams in the slime, oppressive heat, and glitzy dressed harlots that clamored for attention near the base in Vietnam. Nancy suffered through her own reality in my absence but steeled up to face me down when I returned and used her as my whipping boy for all the things that went wrong in my life following the war. School had changed, and while I attempted to pick up where I left off in getting a business education, I found my interests had waned, and my ability to respond to the tasks of classrooms and tests was not the same. Nancy paid the price. The GI Bill was an attractive way to supplement our household income, but "you don't get the pay if you don't make the grade". Fortunately, there were no little Robinettes to worry about. We had held off in having kids at first, thinking it to our advantage until I had completed my education and gotten on in the world of work. Then, after Nam, we tried in the few times our bodies agreed with our minds, or at least our lusts, but failed. Both of us blamed it on the *God Damned War*, but I knew there was something more personal. Nancy put up with it – and me – for another three years. Three years of my bitching and complaining about her, my life, my inability to bring about change that I sought, what the war had done to me, and even the dog! The poor harmless mutt, seeking only to be loved, ended up getting the boot.

I drained off my parents in Nancy's absence. They were willing to do it out of a feeling of compassion for what they perceived as results of an unjust war, an imperfect marriage, and love for their youngest son. They held off comparing the successes of my older brother Edward who seemed able to put all the marbles in the right place, knowing my fragile temperament at once again hearing how Edward had made another score. Now, their help had no green behind it. I had gotten from them all the financial help they would offer, and it was up to me as an adult to find my own way in life. I think they call it *tough love.*

The streets have their place, but they are not the solution to a troubled soul. I learned to cope, use offered homeless resources when I could, withstand the absence of love, warmth and an occasional Heath bar, and seek a shred of self-respect when I compared my existence to that of the other souls I shared this patch of life with.

Then I met Sally. She was pretty. She was alive. She seemed to have purpose, and she seemed to see something in me that even I could not detect. For her, I tried. She brought out a smile my face had not used in years. I followed up on a job she suggested at the lumber yard, and guess what? They hired me as though they also saw something in me. It wasn't the job I would have wanted, but it was a job and it paid me enough to say farewell to the streets. It helped to seal the deal with Sally, and she offered to share her small apartment with me. We were a couple!

You notice I said, "were a couple", because that's what people perceived about us for a long time. Then I became the real me, no longer seeing Sally as that someone special, no longer treating that job at the lumber yard as being anything more than drudgery. I can't even remember how long it took, but the everlooming shadow was becoming suffocating. My downward spiral wasn't taken lightly by Sally. She really cared for me and tried her best to set aside the outbursts of temper, but it was the raging nightmares that scared the hell out of her. She was strong to a point but didn't know how to kill or at least understand these dragons I had brought home from the war. My darkness was growing to the extent that I considered checking out of it all. Was there anything more to life? And then I was introduced to VWG.

The Veterans Writing Group of San Diego interested me at first because of a friend who shared some of my same experiences in Nam.

I don't know why I let him talk me into going one Saturday to their monthly meeting in Oceanside, but I'm glad I did. It wasn't a Vietnam veteran that captured my attention, not even a veteran, but the widow of veteran whose PTSD drove him out of this world through suicide. Something unknown to me brought her here, now, today, into my fragile mental state. Listening to Alexa relate to what she had gone through in her marriage translated loud and clear, five by five, into what it must have been like for Nancy and for Sally to live with me. I was a real bastard! Now that I knew *it*, what was I willing to do about *it*?

That's why, when Sally said, "*Get off your ass, you lazy son of a bitch*", I headed for the desk and my computer. I have already written two small books, and contributed several small articles for veteran oriented printings, but now I am determined to write "*something of substance*". Not that I'm a writer of note, but I have learned that being a writer requires me to be a reader as well. And read I do, constantly. The bad dreams are still there, but somehow my writing seems to make me more capable of living with them until they subside. It also must be making Sally more capable of living with me, as she is now to be the mother of my first child, and perhaps the first of many.

STILL IN THE FIGHT
Don Gomez

It was eerily dark when we left the relative safety of the slapped together wooden shacks that lined the airstrip. The whir of awakening propellers greeted us as we ran across the blacktop single file toward our bird. As I ran past my Chief Warrant Officer, he gave the back of my Kevlar a light smack for good measure. A little something to take the edge off, I suppose.

We always flew at night. We only flew at night. Any other time of day would have been a suicide mission, all those eyes on the ground waiting for us to be daring enough to get within range. We never gave 'em the satisfaction though.

I climbed aboard and covered down, just like Gunner had told me to when he slapped my helmet moments earlier. On this particular flight, that meant that I'd be sitting with my back against the wall of the aircraft, as opposed to sitting in the center and facing outboard. It occurred to me that my back was literally against the wall as we undertook to foray out into hazardous and hostile country.

I gazed idly about the bird's dingy gray interior, hoping to find something that would draw my interest enough to ease the discomfort and boredom I was sure the long flight would bring. I found nothing. Those helos were built for function, not aesthetics.

Yep, an hour and a half ride from Fallujah to TQ in a CH-46 was no picnic. There were no flight attendants offering cocktails. Hell, no one even offered me a bag of peanuts. Not that that mattered; I wasn't hungry anyway.

After the pilot had signaled the "the good to go" and gotten clearance to take off, we were under way—pitching across a dark and seemingly deserted landscape toward yet another dreary beige bastion of Western imperialism in that land of sun and dust.

About twenty minutes into our voyage, I had finally managed to become somewhat comfortable (or had resigned myself to discomfort, I'm not sure which). I was slumped down very ungracefully in the thin retractable seat and had just closed my eyes in an attempt at sleep when I heard a dull thud resound against the chopper's fuselage somewhere behind and to the left of me.

Before I could even assess the cause of the noise, I heard a second, a third, and then many more such noises. They seemed to be striking every part of the craft, which then began to vibrate from the constant barrage. It sounded like dozens of hammers wielded by enraged blacksmiths, all taking cracks at an anvil.

As it dawned on me what was occurring, our tail gunner was diving into action behind the .50 caliber machine gun that adorned the bird's flank. Apparently, this was not his first time before the forge. But it sure was mine!

At just that moment, my wits were shattered by the deafening thud of a large caliber round directly behind my head. The ringing in my ears made me keenly aware that, were it not for the metal walls of our craft, I would have been left without need of the helmet that adorned my frazzled melon.

Every instinct I had was screaming at me to do something—to not just sit and hope for the best, but there was nothing I could do. I was bound by protocol to "stand the hell by" and trust others to do their duty.

Paranoia and fear washed over me then. So, this was it? Every memory, dream, and aspiration I'd ever had would come crashing down in a heap in a desert on the other side of the world from where my memories, dreams, and aspirations had lived.

I looked around at the others, the noise of the big gun echoing in my head and resounding around the fuselage of the helicopter. They all looked so calm. Were they really calm, or were they just paralyzed by their own fear? Did I look like them, or did the worry register on my face alone?

If it did, did I have the right? They would all go just the same as I. Besides, I had volunteered to be here, here in the Marine Corps. Here, wherever in the world here currently was, wherever they sent me.

At least I'd die a hero.

Old men in overalls and John Deere caps who don't understand "my type" would bow their heads in tribute to my sacrifice, nonetheless. Meanwhile, well-meaning young men in olive drab coats and black berets with red stars sown into them would mock the death of yet another fascist tool. I may die a hero, but a hero to whom? My own convictions never factoring into history's portrayal of what I lived and died for.

As I paused to reflect on what that actually meant, I became aware of a decrease in volume. The incessant pinging of metal on metal was slackening. Before long, it was too far off to be heard. Nothing in the actions or demeanor of the crew indicated that I had anything more to fear other than a renewed outburst of firepower from another source somewhere farther along our route. It seemed we had come through it all and were still aloft.

I think I passed the rest of the flight in stunned silence, but I can't be sure, because I was definitely in shock. All that I recall is touching down on the airstrip at TQ and being damned glad to be back on the ground. I knew that I had the return trip to look forward to, but, in that brief moment, nothing else mattered. All that was important was that for now, I was still here, I was still alive, and I was still in the fight!

THE CHAPEL THAT NEVER WAS
Frank Ritter

Robert Fennell, my then father-in-law, was a Twentieth Century Fox Studio vice president. During the 1940s he was also the studio's representative to the War Department, and later the Pentagon. He told me this story

In the months following Japan's Pearl Harbor attack, the Japanese prepared for their invasion of Australia by invading New Guinea, which sits just north of Australia's eastern half. Then, on July 1, 1942, they invaded the Solomon Islands to Australia's east and began creating an airfield out of the jungle on Guadalcanal. The Allies' theater commander, General Douglas MacArthur, planned to defend Australia against a Japanese invasion by invading New Guinea, but first, something had to be done about the Japanese airfield on Guadalcanal, which would be sitting on his flank when he attacked New Guinea. To that end, in August 1942, Marines attacked Guadalcanal to capture the airfield.

Richard Tregaskis, a war correspondent covering the Guadalcanal battle, promptly began writing a memoir of the fight. His book, Guadalcanal Diary, was published on January 1, 1943, while the battle was still raging. Twentieth Century Fox instantly purchased the book's movie rights. Bob Fennell made the necessary arrangements for the movie, starring Preston Foster, William Bendix, and Anthony Quinn, to be filmed on the Marine's newly built Camp Pendleton, about a hundred miles south of the Fox studio.

The filming was fast and furious, beginning in mid-May, 1943, and wrapping two and a half months later near the end of July. Marines on the base at the time were cast as extras in most of the scenes. The movie released on November 5, 1943. Darryl F. Zanuck, the Fox Studio head, had pushed the filming and post-production hard so that the movie would be a birthday present to the Marine Corps, which celebrated its birthday on November 10. Guadalcanal Diary showed the public that America's Marines were taking the war to the enemy, teaching the invincible and never-defeated Japanese a thing or two about combat. The picture was loved by critics and the public alike, and it was a tremendous hit.

By 1947–1948 the war was over, and Zanuck wanted to show his appreciation to the Marines for the movie's success by holding a cast and crew party. He sent Bob Fennell to Camp Pendleton with the name of every Marine who had appeared in the movie, no matter how briefly. Bob met with the base commander, and while they chatted, the list was scoured to determine where the Marines were so they could be rounded up and flown to Hollywood at Fox's expense. They were going to be wined, dined, and honored at a huge Hollywood Gala party.

A young officer quietly entered the room where Bob and the general were talking. Bob told me he could see that the young man was desperately trying to hold himself together. He stood at attention and set the list on the general's desk, saying, "General, not one marine on that list survived the war. They all died."

Bob blurted out in disbelief, "Not one survived?"

"No, sir, not one."

Bob uttered, "My God!" as he crossed himself. He then said, "General, may I use your phone? Zanuck needs to know this now."

Darryl Zanuck quietly listened to Bob's sad news, and then said, "Ask the general what they need."

Bob relayed the request, and the general thoughtfully replied, "A chapel."

Bob told me that Zanuck had been deeply impacted by the news, quietly, sadly saying, "Tell the general to pick a location. The construction crew will be there in the morning to build that chapel."

Bob told me this story some 20 years later. With great pride, he talked about how Twentieth Century Fox Studios, as a tribute to those fallen marines, had built a chapel on Camp Pendleton out of rock, large enough to seat 250 people.

In 2003, I moved to Oceanside, California, near Camp Pendleton, and began asking Marines about the chapel. None knew of such a chapel. I asked one of the base chaplains who told me there was no chapel on the base constructed from rock. I truly believed my father-in-law and pushed harder. I contacted the base Historical Society who confirmed that there was no chapel on the base constructed of rock. However, the historian added, their very old, dilapidated and nearly falling down Ranch House Chapel had been completely restored sometime during the 1947–1948 period. She stated that the chapel had been built around 1808 and there were no records relating to the restoration project. No records of where the money came from nor the construction company that did the work.

The only thing they knew for certain was that it had been restored and that the actor Anthony Quinn had donated eight stained-glass windows and some other artifacts for it. The historian told me that Quinn donated the windows because during the filming of Guadalcanal Diary, he, being a Catholic, had often attended Mass at the chapel. Subsequently, in preparation for writing this piece, I have read online that the Historical Society now says, "Movie studios donated $9,000 for the chapel's restoration."

I have been a licensed private investigator for over 40 years and I have solved many, many cases by asking myself: How can all the witnesses, who are telling somewhat different or even completely different stories, be telling the truth and yet we somehow arrive at this unnatural conclusion? In the chapel's case, how could my father-in-law be telling me the truth, and at the same time, people in the know are telling me the exact opposite?

I believe the resolution to the conundrum lies with Anthony Quinn and the stained-glass windows. How would Anthony Quinn know to supply stained-glass windows to the old chapel? He lived in Beverly Hills, a distance of at least 120 miles north of Camp Pendleton, so it is highly unlikely he popped down there to go to Mass. It is also highly unlikely that during the four to five years between the filming of Guadalcanal Diary and the chapel's restoration, he was somehow keeping tabs on the old chapel. So, if there was no Fox Studio involvement in the restoration, how did Quinn learn about it? How did he learn about the chapel's need for windows? Somebody had to tell him. However, if my conjecture that Fox Studios did the restoration is correct and given that Anthony Quinn was under contract to Fox Studios and Darryl Zanuck, it's not much of a stretch to think that Quinn learned about the chapel undergoing restoration from Zanuck.

I think that once the general began the process of locating a suitable site for the new chapel, someone suggested to the general that instead of building a new one, would Fox Studios consider restoring their current, nearly 140-year-old dilapidated Ranch House Chapel?

I believe that when the Fox construction crew arrived at Camp Pendleton, they obtained Zanuck's approval to restore the Ranch

House Chapel instead of building a new one, and that's what they did. That would explain why the base Historical Society would have no clear record of how the restoration was paid for and who did it, but knows it was done.

In the beginning, Zanuck would have notified the cast and crew about the planned party. However, after his telephone conversation with Bob, he most likely told the movie's major stars, at least, about all of the marines in the cast dying and the restoring of the old chapel. That would explain how Anthony Quinn knew to donate the stained-glass windows and other artifacts.

My father-in-law had done what he had been told to do. He had made the necessary arrangements for a chapel to be built out of rock, and therefore would have been out of the loop regarding anything more about it. So, to the day he died, he believed that a rock chapel had been built on Camp Pendleton.

And until a few years ago, so did I.

A RECYCLED BIBLE
Chuck Norberg

Upon completion of two years of flight training and receiving my wings from Naval Aviation Flight School, Pensacola, Florida in 1987, my parents gave me a pocket size New Testament lovingly inscribed, "To Chuck, from Mom and Dad with all our prayers." I began my Navy flying career by placing it in my flight suit breast pocket, and always thereafter, I would do a pre-flight check making sure that the Bible was with me. This became routine for me each time I climbed into my helicopter, and I never flew without it.

After some years had passed and several deployments served, Christmas 2005 found me packing for my January deployment. Much to my dismay, I could not find my Bible. I rummaged through many packed boxes from my completion of a two-year tour as Squadron Commander at Naval Air Station North Island. The Bible was not to be found.

My parents were visiting for the holidays, and they shared in the anguish of my lost Bible. However, they returned home a few days after Christmas, and soon thereafter, I received a package in the mail. To my surprise, it was another New Testament—but not a new one. It, too, was inscribed, "To Chuck, from Mom and Dad with all our prayers." It was a New Testament that had belonged to my dad, also Chuck. His parents had given it to him when he joined the Navy in the Korean War. This Bible from my grandparents was very special to me also.

I happily packed the 'recycled' Bible and left for my deployment as Air Boss on the USS Tarawa, an amphibious assault ship for all missions and combat operations. I knew that my parents would not only be praying for me, but also for God's love and protection for the entire crew as we served our country. I did find my 'misplaced' Bible that my parents had given me. I have placed both of them in my Navy Memoir Box.

OH, SAY CAN YOU SEE
W. Paul Jameson

I was a petty officer in the operations department of our submarine. Before getting underway from Norfolk, Virginia, to cross the Atlantic for the Mediterranean, I was tasked to round up spare parts for the ETs, the Radiomen and my own rate, the Sonarmen. I was also offered a driver job while we were in Europe, providing I got an international driver's license, including my picture.

I quickly changed into my dress blues uniform, got a government car, and zoomed off base. I had many stops to make. It took too long, but I was determined to get everything, including that photo and driver's license. I succeeded, and with paper bags full of electronic do-dads, I raced back to the base.

When I arrived, the guard at the gate asked, "Are you the guy everyone's looking for?"

"What?" I asked worried.

"You had better get a move on buddy. Your boat's getting underway right now."

"What!" And I raced to the submarine tender.

A chief met me at the gangway and said, "Just give me the keys and get going."

I ran up the gangway into the innards of the massive ship, immediately got lost, and yelled into the air, "Can someone tell me how to get to the other side of this ship? My sub's getting underway!"

A couple guys came over and almost pulled me through passageways and up and down ladders until we got to the other side. My boat had already started moving. All lines had been thrown over except one. The stern was out away from the large tender, and seeing that I yelled to the guys on the bridge, "I'm here. I'm here, captain, I'm here!"

The Chief of the Boat standing on the after deck ran over to the side of the sail and cried out too, "Jameson's here, captain!" The skipper looked back from his perch and then gave orders to the Conn to move the stern back towards the side of the tender.

When there was less than a 20-foot gap between my submarine and the tender, the Chief of the Boat yelled, "Jump Jameson! We'll catch you."

I threw the paper bags full of the requisitioned parts over to some guys on deck, then got back as far as I could inside the large ship—I think I was inside a mess hall—ran as fast as I could, leaped through the air, and landed on one of the ballast tanks. Two guys grabbed my flailing arms to keep me from falling into the water and pulled me up on deck.

"Where the hell have you been?" the chief asked. "You almost missed movement."

"Sorry chief. I had to get those parts."

He shook his head, and I laid below while the last line was thrown over. Our captain had made Commander and was therefore made senior officer present afloat in our small flotilla of four submarines that would cross the Atlantic in formation. It was April, the weather was great, and we had no exercises to do while crossing, so we just traveled in a straight line on the surface all the way. The only momentous event for me was seeing a blue whale.

Our first landfall was Lisbon, Portugal. Like many sailors, we simply walked the streets and went on tours. We stopped at a restaurant called April in Portugal, heard a lady sing the Fado, and learned to shut up when she was singing. The Fado is almost a religion with the Portuguese and you had better be quiet while the performer is pouring out his or her heart about some story of great importance in their culture. We also went to a bullfight on their opening day and saw men wrestle the bull. One was gored and died later.

The next day we entered the Mediterranean through the Straits of Gibraltar. From then on, our little flotilla of four submarines dispersed, each one heading toward its assignment in the fleet. Ours was to call in at Naples where we met a bunch of charming, personable boys begging for money just outside the gate. We had been warned about them, but I thought, what can they do? I can take care of myself. So we waded into the mass of kids, laughed at their forcefulness, acquiesced a little and forked over a few dollars and walked on. Then I checked my wallet and noted that my 20-dollar bill was missing and exclaimed, "They stole my twenty!" My friends laughed. Then I looked at my watch to check the time, but it too was gone. "My watch is gone! How'd they get it off my wrist?" and my friends laughed again. Welcome to Italy!

For the most part, Europe was, while not dull, not overly exciting either. Pompeii was fascinating, but I think the most interesting place was Malta. Little Malta is a microcosm of many of the significant events in European history. The Apostle Paul was shipwrecked there. Christian symbols carved in ancient stones testify to his immense influence.

And there were Roman aqueducts, Roman sculpture, and walls and forts and ancient moats that are now roads and parking lots. We visited St. John's Co-Cathedral, where bible stories were painted on the ceiling in 3D above hand-carved walls. Never saw anything like it. The floor itself was graves of Crusader Knights, each with his coat of arms in marble. And off to the side were small sanctuaries or chapels with altars for each of the nations who sent knights to fight in the crusades. Malta was a sovereign country, but it kept a strong British naval presence. We tied our boat up along a pier behind a British submarine, thinking it was kind of cool, until we found out those Brits were totally nuts. They spent all their time either getting drunk or insuring they stayed drunk.

And it became apparent that they considered us to be brothers in arms because, while they were subjects of the Queen, we were former British subjects. Therefore, in their minds, that meant our submarine was their submarine too. So whenever we went to eat in our mess, it was half full of drunken British sailors. Okay, we thought, we can play the same game. So, we found out when they ate and showed up in their mess to chow down.

Then the trading began. Uniforms for uniforms and eventually flags for flags until one day when the British captain had to get underway, he discovered there was not a single British flag left on board. All his flags were the Stars and Stripes. He sent a sailor over to get one of their flags back.

One night my friend and I met two Brits on liberty. As usual, they were drunk. Now, of course, our guys drank too, but for some reason, the Brits didn't seem to have much self-control. We, on the other hand, were almost threatened with life in the brig if we messed up.

We flagged down a taxi and all piled in. One Brit was in front, and my friend and I shared the back seat with the other Brit who was drinking a liter bottle of beer. While the taxi was en route, he finished and decided to throw the bottle out the window. Problem: the window was closed. He threw it anyway, breaking the bottle and the window. I leaned over to my friend and whispered, "We've got to get away from these guys. When the taxi stops, run." The taxi did stop and the angry driver started yelling. I opened the door, and we bolted to the left. The Brits took my cue, bolted to the right, and the poor taxi driver was left alone, screaming curses into the night.

We operated with the fleet in exercises that I don't remember, but I guess it was all essential. Of course, naval exercises are seldom understood by the rank and file. We were told to go here or there, submerge, do this or that and on and on. Only flag and senior officers back in some room someplace saw the whole picture and understood the purpose. But I guess we and the rest of the ships had done a smashing good job because the admiral decided we needed to have a party—a picnic on some remote beach. The secluded beach chosen lay at the head of a desolate bay in Sardinia. An announcement said, "We're going to have a picnic … with some other ships."

The day came. The other submarines that peeled off when we entered the Med returned, and we were four again. We entered the bay to see a couple destroyers already anchored. Well, we thought, this is going to be kind of a big deal. We dropped anchor. Boats came over and collected those of us who didn't have duty. Then they went back for the cooks and food; lots and lots of food.

Different ships contributed footballs, baseballs and volleyballs and nets, all the stuff for playing games. Fires were started, and the cooks got busy. And then boats started arriving with cases and cases of beer. Wow! Beer! This is a *really* big deal: beer, games, and barbecues. But we weren't allowed to drink yet and had to wait for the food, so I lay down on the beach with a few friends. Others started ball games, and we just waited. Someone had a large radio and tuned it to the

Armed Forces Radio Network, which played patriotic and martial music.

And then, what we thought was a really big deal became a huge deal.

As the marshal music played, more U.S. Navy ships began to hove into sight around a point; first a destroyer and then another and another, and a cruiser, and more ships of all kinds. We had never seen anything like it in our lives. Guys playing games stopped. Cooks, bent over pots and grills, stood up straight. The men who were lying down rose to their feet. Hundreds of young men all over the beach stopped what they were doing and stared.

A Navy man may see some ships tied up to piers in a harbor, or a few around his ship while at sea, but ships are generally not together in large numbers. This was different though; the fleet began arriving. It was the first time I, and perhaps any of my shipmates had seen such a sight.

While those ships entered the bay quietly, majestically, and proudly—with the sun reflecting off of their hulls and high bridges and gun turrets—the national anthem began to play on that radio sitting on the beach, "Oh say can you see..." And while standing and motionless, staring at the magnificent spectacle, I thought, "God, we are a great nation."

That day I was genuinely proud to be a Navy man and an American.

AUTHORS' BIOGRAPHIES

Anissia Asencio

Joseph Ashby is a native Coloradoan. The military has been a part of his life since he enlisted in the Navy at the age of 17 during the Korean War. In the 12 years that followed, he served as an aircrew "twidgit" (aviation electronics) radio/radar/ecm member, was recalled during the Berlin Crisis, and then went to Officer Candidate School. After time off for "good behavior," Joe tried the Air Force through the Air National Guard as an operations tech and rose to 1st Sergeant, Chief Master Sergeant, and Command Chief. He retired with nearly 30 years of service. Since then, he has been actively involved in veterans' services. He has also had careers in communications marketing, product management, firefighting, and over 20 years in training management with FEMA. A father of three daughters, Joe resides in Oceanside, California, where he still pursues military interests.

Dr. Vernita Black is a veteran who retired after serving 21 years in the United States Navy. During her time in the military, Dr. Black earned her doctorate in Education Counseling Psychology. Her work in education, training, stress management and drug and alcohol education led her to research alcohol and substance use among adolescents.
Dr. Black is the author of *Parent's Perceptions of their adolescents' attitude towards substance use: By ethnic differences* and is also the author of *Life's reflections: A collection of poems on serenity, peace, and faith*. Her latest published work is titled *"The Invisible Wounds of Stress: Inside and Out."* Dr. Black discovered through faith, hope, peace, and happiness that all things are possible in the midst of it all.

Robert (Bob) Bowman grew up in a small village in eastern Pennsylvania. While in high school he enlisted in the Navy Reserve. He discovered that he liked the Navy and was soon offered an opportunity to compete for a fleet appointment to the Naval Academy. While a midshipman he made a summer cruise on a submarine. That convinced him to pursue a career in submarines. Twenty years later, a submarine-related tour of duty as a Navy bureaucrat in the Pentagon convinced him it was time to try his hand at a civilian career. That career, as a telecommunications /technology manager for a large bank in Seattle, was cut short by an accident that left his wife disabled. He served as her full-time caregiver until she passed 22 years later. Bob now lives in a retirement community in Elizabethtown, PA where he is remarried and enjoys travel and occasional writing. He has one daughter who lives in Colorado.

Robert John Buck served in the USMC from 1964 to 1966 with the famed 1st battalion, 9th Marines, known as The Walking Dead. He attended Moorpark College, acquiring a degree in business. He worked a widely varied career in business and developed a taste for creative writing while formulating colorful ad copy for various launchings of business promos.

Tom Calabrese is a Marine Corps veteran who saw combat in Vietnam 1969-1970 as a combat infantryman. He also served the Marine Corps, Navy and Army Reserves. He is a graduate of UC Berkeley with a bachelor's degree in Communications and Public Policy.
A prolific screenwriter and action/adventure fiction writer, he is the author of the novel *Some of the Best,* which is available on Amazon and has written over 200 short stories. His stories can be read in thevistapress.com every Sunday.

Robert Caudill grew up just outside Detroit, Michigan, and joined the Marine Corps when he was 24 years old. He served with HMM364, "The Purple Foxes," for four deployments during 2004-2010 as an aviation ordnance man, fixing machine guns and loading counter measure flares. He also participated in casualty evacuation, which resulted in his medical retirement in 2012 with Post Traumatic Stress. He and Erin Holmes co-founded I Journey, a wellness center that offers restorative yoga, sound healing, and more, free of charge to veterans, the elderly, and emergency responders, and on a sliding scale fee to the community.

J. Randall Davis has a BA in English from Stanford University, an MA in English from University of California Irvine, and an MSW from USC, where he was enrolled in the Military Social Work and Veteran Services Program. In the eight years since graduating from USC's program in 2011, Randy has had various roles in the Transition Assistance Program at Camp Pendleton. In addition to his career working with service members, he has taught composition at MiraCosta College for eighteen years. Randy edited Veterans' Writing Group's (VWG's) first book, co-edited VWG's second book, and is a co-editor of this, VWG's third book. Collaborating with VWG's members in the production of those three publications has been one of the great honors of Randy's life.

Maria Galvan-Dupree was born in San Mateo, CA and raised in Southern CA. She is the daughter of Atanacio and Carolina Galvan. Her father passed when she was 13 years old and the oldest of 5 siblings. Her single parent was instrumental in parenting her children to grow up educated, independent, and hard-working, productive individuals. Maria Enlisted into the Active Army serving three years with 127 th Signal Bn at Fort Ord 7 th ID in Monterey CA. In 1992 she joined C Co 240 th SIgnal BN in the CA National Guard. With prior service, Maria eventually was commissioned into the Medical Field. She completed her command time on active duty with E Co Med 540 MSB at The National Training Center at Fort Irwin CA 2005. Maria spent the rest of her military service with the MED Det then with HHC 40th ID Los Alamitos California. Maria graduated with a degree in Counseling Psychology and worked with San Diego County for 13 years as a Mental Health Clinician. She is retired as a Major from service in 2012. Maria worked with combat Veterans for five years at a Vet Center before retiring from her civilian job. She is a 40 th ID Alumni. Her love of helping her fellow Veterans has led her to write her experiences.

Brenda Fonseca served in the Navy from 2012 to 2018 as an electronics technician. She is grateful for all the life experiences and opportunities the Navy offered her. Brenda is now happily living in Oceanside, California, with her husband, son, two dogs and cat.

Tom J. Foreman enlisted in the navy in 1939 for six years. He served slightly more than the time he signed on for because of the intervention of World War II. Following his release from active duty in 1945, he took an entry level position as a file clerk with the Bank of America in San Diego. He retired from Bank of America 37 years later as a Vice President after numerous promotions and several moves. He resides in Escondido, CA. with his second wife. Tom will celebrate his 100th birthday next year.

Glen Foss served as a junior naval officer from 1966-70 during the Vietnam conflict. His duty assignments in the western Pacific included a diesel-electric submarine and a mobile inshore undersea warfare unit. After retiring from his civilian career as seagoing operations superintendent for the scientific Deep-Sea Drilling Project and Ocean Drilling Program, he taught oceanography and geology courses at local community colleges. He currently does some freelance editing and writes mostly fiction—for entertainment and "mental calisthenics."

Shara French served 20 years in the Marine Corps, retiring as a Gunnery Sergeant. Ammunition Technician trained, she also was a Leadership Program Coordinator, facilitating Dr. Stephen Covey's "*7 Habits of Highly Effective People*" workshops, prior to retiring in 2001. After retirement, Shara pursued higher education, culminating in an MA in Literature and Writing Studies from California State University San Marcos in 2017. Her published works include the poems "Growing Meaning like Bean Seeds," included in the university chapbook of May 2010, and "Molly Ann," included in the university chapbook of May 2017. Her latest published work is her Master's thesis, titled "Worlds Apart: An Evolving Woman, One Female Marine's Assimilation into Patriarchal Spaces, and the Grief Coda, including Critical Introduction." Shara is a member of the Woman Marine Association, as well as a lifetime member of the Veterans of Foreign Wars.

Garry G. Garretson received his air crew wings and other air medals serving in the United States Navy from 1965 to 1969 as a Second-Class Petty Officer. He flew transportation and early warning flights in support of fleet units in the Gulf of Tonkin and Southeast Asia from 1967–1969. His unit was part of the famed "Typhoon Trackers," which penetrated and tracked typhoons throughout the Pacific Ocean. He was an electronics technician and an in-flight radioman. Garry retired after a 40-year career with a Fortune 500 company, ARAMARK. Formerly a Marshfield (MA) School Committee member and Parks and Recreation
Commissioner in Massachusetts, Garry stays busy as a member of several nonprofit boards supporting children, the Vista (CA) Planning Commission, and North Coast Church. He is married with three children and one grandson.

Don Gomez is a Marine Corps veteran and small business owner. Don also currently serves as Communications Director of National Veterans Group, a nonprofit organization that analyzes and reports on legislation that impacts the military community. He is passionate about making a difference for veterans and military families and is amongst those leading the charge to repatriate our deported veterans and ensure professional licensure reciprocity for military spouses. Don resides in Oceanside, CA with his wife Michelle.

Lawrence J. Klumas enlisted in the United States Air Force in January 1961 and retired from continuous active duty in August 1987 as a Colonel. As an enlisted man, he was trained as a GCA ground radar repairman; as an officer, he was in the Civil Engineering Corps. He was stationed at Tan Son Nhut Air Base in Saigon, Vietnam, when the Tet Offensive was waged. He has been writing since attending college in the 1950s. Some recent poems have been published in JerryJazzMusician and in the Episcopal Diocese Messenger. Lawrence passed away in 2019.

Chuck Norberg grew up in Springfield, Virginia and graduated from Virginia Polytechnic Institute and State University in 1983. He went to Pensacola, Florida and received his commission from Navy Officer Candidate School and completed two years at Naval Flight School at NAS Whiting Field, Florida. His flying career began with the CH46 helicopters before the Navy's new helicopter, SH60B Seahawk. He ended his 28-year career in 2012, having accrued over 4000 flight hours and receiving two air medals while serving on eight deployments and three combat tours, including three years as Air Boss on the USS Tarawa and two years as Squadron Commander at NAS, North Island. He transitioned from active duty to his second career at the Naval Information Warfare Systems Command (SPAWAR).

He lives in Scripps Ranch with his wife, Erin. His interests are mostly centered around the activities of his four children—a son and daughter who are very active at Scripps Ranch High School, a son who attends the Miami University in Ohio and a daughter, a recent graduate of CA Poly. He enjoys walking and bike rides with his dog, Skipper.

Pete Peterson's quest for baseball's Hall of Fame ended when he could hit neither the fast ball nor the curve. His first published story appeared in *Seventeen Magazine* when he was seventeen and in Marine Corps Boot Camp. This earned him $35.00 and two hours standing at attention in front of the drill instructor's hut yelling, "My name is Private Peterson, not Ernest Hemingway."

Pete's short story collection, *After Midnight* (Pallamary Publishing) is available on Amazon. His work has been featured in many publications including, *Leatherneck, Dead Mule School of Southern Literature, Charles Carter - A Working Anthology, Raven's Perch, Stoneslide Collective, Scarlet Leaf Review and Deadly Writer's Patrol.* After a day dangling participles, ambushing nouns and slaying little darlings, he's been known to eat popcorn, drink Diet Pepsis and roar obscenities when his beloved St. Louis Cardinals lose a ball game. He facilitates a twice monthly read & critique group at the Escondido Library. He can be reached at **www.rlpetepeterson.com**.

Captain Ron Pickett is a retired naval aviator with over 250 combat missions and 500 carrier landings. He was the commanding officer of a squadron and a human resource management center. His 90-plus articles have appeared in numerous publications. Ron's areas of specialization are leadership and management development and customer relations, among others. He enjoys writing fiction and has published five books: *Perfect Crimes – I Got Away with It, Discovering Roots, Getting Published, EMPATHS,* and *Sixty Odd Short Stories.*

Dante' Puccetti enlisted in the Army and became an artillery surveyor. He was stationed in Vietnam at the HHB, Fourth Division Artillery at Camp Enary, Pleiku, from June 1968 – March 1969. He received a BA in psychology in 1986, and then worked as a counselor, data manager, and research and statistical analyst in the Alcohol Treatment Unit at the Veterans Administration Medical Center in Loma Linda, California. With Dr Michael Chang and Dr Paul Yamaguchi, Dante' co-authored a paper published in *The Journal of Alcohol Studies* titled "Split Level Validity of Treatment Compliance in an Alcohol Treatment Program." Dante' was a recent staff member at Southern California News. Organ of the Sports Car Club of America. Part of his memoir was published in *Exiting Vietnam*, authored by Michael Eggleston. Dante' is a member of Eggleston's writing review staff.

Ray Resler was never one to sit still for very long, Ray moved from his birthplace in Yankton, South Dakota to Sioux City, Iowa, at an early age. He initially worked as a weights and measure inspector for various railroads until World War II intervened. Serving with the U. S. Coast Guard, he was sent to the South Pacific on a Landing Ship Tank (LST). His position was "topside" as a Fire Controlman.
Following his three years of service, he returned home to resume his employment as a railroad inspector. Ray then attended the Montana School of Mines, the University of Utah, and the University of California, Berkeley, receiving his B.S and M.S. in Geophysics. He accepted an offer to teach at Grossmont College in 1961 as part of the founding faculty. His "claim to fame" was leading field trips to Mt. Whitney and the Grand Canyon. Ray has traveled to 72 countries, including Thailand, where he maintained a home for ten years.

Ray has resided in San Diego since retiring from Grossmont College in 1995. His family includes a son, two daughters, and two granddaughters.

Bruce Rowe honed his writing skills as a business reporter and corporate communications pro. Now his business, StorySetFree, focuses on helping authors write their books, including ghostwriting, editing, website development, SEO, and publishing guidance. His writing experience includes book collaboration/ghostwriting, articles, web content, broadcast copy, video scripts, presentations, and short stories. Recent projects include editorial review and editing of a novel series, editing and formatting an illustrated biography, and ghostwriting two personal finance books.

Frank Ritter is a multiple-award-winning playwright, a novelist, and the author of non-fiction books. He was a squadron commander in the USAF Auxiliary, Civil Air Patrol, holding the rank of captain. He has been a private investigator (PI) in California since 1975. As such, he has investigated injury cases that have won over $500,000,000 for the injured parties, has provided enough evidence for convictions in four homicides, and has trained PIs all over the country. Frank has published 23 books and seven plays of which five have been produced on the stage.

Frank Sutton, MD Frank served in the U. S. Army in Europe during World War II. Following his discharge, he attended medical school and was a physician in private practice in Pasadena, California for over 37 years. He was a strong supporter of the Veterans' Writing Group and is greatly missed.

Mark Steinberg was born in 1919. His father was a small businessman and he was raised in a middle-class home He received a Junior College Certificate in --- and joined the Army Air Corps He completed pilot training and then went for advanced training in the B26 medium bomber. He spent a year flying from North Africa bombing targets in Italy and Germany. Following his release from active duty he taught mathematics at the Junior High school level. During the summers he worked at a restaurant in Yosemite Park. After his retirement he enjoyed the beauty of California hiking the Pacific Crest Trail. He currently resides in Escondido and is a proud veteran of World War II.

Luz Helena (Stacey) Thompson, USMC Veteran. Co-founder of Veterans Recovery Project, enlisted in the United States Marine Corps at age 17. She volunteered for her first overseas duty station to Okinawa, Japan in 1999. Shortly after her arrival to Okinawa, Stacey experienced sexual harassment in her workplace. In December 1999, she was raped by her superior Non-Commissioned Officer (NCO). As a result of reporting the rape, she was retaliated against and separated from the Marines with an Other Than Honorable discharge. Over a decade later Stacey became a public advocate for survivors of military sexual assault.

Although a disabled veteran herself, Stacey is also her husband's full-time caregiver. In 2013, Stacey joined Senator Barbara Boxer in Los Angeles where she shared her story publicly for the first time. Her powerful speech led her to be invited by Senator Kirsten Gillibrand in 2014 to speak in Washington, DC, in support of the Military Justice Improvement Act. Stacey graduated with honors and has a Master of Science Degree from the California University of Pennsylvania. She was featured in Veterans Coming Home, a documentary in conjunction with PBS of short films which depict the struggles disabled veterans face after coming home and reintegrating back into society. In January 2016, after four years of litigation, Stacey received a discharge upgrade from the Department of Defense which finally acknowledged her honorable military service and she is now receiving her veteran's benefits. Her tenacity and perseverance is apparent in not only her character but, in her advocacy work as well. Stacey can gracefully articulate her experiences with MST and PTSD offering a unique understanding from both the veteran and caregiver perspective. Her success and commitment to advocacy thus far is certainly an indication of things to come.

Leif K. Thorsten served in the United States Marine Corps from 1968-1993. He is a Combat Veteran, having served in the Vietnam War during

1969-1970. He was an enlisted man for 13 years and an officer for 12 years, holding 13 different ranks. After his military career ended, Leif enjoyed working in various fields. He was a cook, a nurseryman, a Corrections Officer with the Western Tidewater Regional Jail, a manager with both Best Buy and JC Penney, and an assistant manager with a chain of retail golf stores in Virginia. At the time of his retirement, Leif was the Department Manager of the Custom Club section of The Golf Warehouse in Wichita, Kansas. He currently resides in Oceanside, California, where he enjoys building scale models, artwork, and, of course, writing.

Art Townley was born and raised in Bromide, Oklahoma. Following his four years' service in the U. S. Navy he attended college and became a high school history teacher. Art continued his education receiving an EDD degree and a teaching position at the University of California at San Bernardo. Art has three textbooks that are used in Graduate School History programs.; he is an Emeritus Professor of U. S. History. Art lives an active life in a retirement community in Rancho Bernardo, CA.

Shirley Turner was married to a Navy Chief Petty Officer for over 40 years. She was a nurse and nurse manager whose specialty was Emergency Medicine. Shirley and her husband raised three children and were the foster parents for numerous children. Shirley's poetry has been widely published and appears in several nurse training manuals.

George Van deWater spent his early days on a small farm in upstate New York. He began flying in 1948 with his father and entered flight training as a Naval Aviation Cadet in early 1954. During three decades as a naval aviator, he served in numerous aircraft squadrons and aircraft carriers, seeing action in the Cuban Missile Crisis and in the Vietnam War. From 1976 to 1980, he was the U.S. Naval Attaché to Thailand, Burma, and Laos. He concluded his 20,000-hour flying career after nineteen years as a pipeline patrol pilot, during which he made 1700 low-altitude crossings of the Southwestern desert between San Diego and El Paso. He has raced sailboats in the Pacific and for seven years sailed in the British Virgin Islands. Since 1985, he has lived with his family in Encinitas, California.

Dusty Ward was born in Peck, Michigan. He joined the Navy at 17 years old and served until the war ended in 1945. After several short-term jobs, he was hired at Sears as an appliance salesman. Many promotions later, he became store manager in San Diego and retired after 35 years with the company.

Charlie Wyatt served in the U. S. Navy 1963-1967. He was deployed to Vietnam for a year as skipper of a Swift Boat. He has had a lifelong love for books and writing and ran his own used bookstore for more than 20 years. He helped found and still participates in two writer's groups. He has had several stories published in various periodicals.

Made in the USA
Lexington, KY
24 November 2019